GET MORE TEA

STORIES AND RECIPES FROM THE WORLD OF TEA

M.C. PEARSON

CONTENTS

INTRODUCTION

This book is part of my ongoing exploration of the world of tea. If you've had the opportunity to read my first book, *Get the Tea,* you would know that I discovered tea much later in life, having been a coffee drinker for my growing years. The only tea I remember in our house growing up was a can of instant iced tea that stayed at the back of our kitchen cupboard for years. Honestly, I don't know what happened to that instant tea.

Living in the Pacific Northwest, coffee was my staple, and how can you blame me? The coffee here is superb, so I only gave tea a little thought. I changed my mind and heart when I tried my first cup of high-quality herbal tea. I've spent the years since that first cup experimenting with teas of all varieties from as many regions as possible. And so began my love affair with tea.

I absorbed as much as I could about the history of tea, the growing, harvesting, manufacturing processes, and of course, the many legends and stories. Learning about the tea plant helped me understand the nuances of making a cup of tea. It gave meaning to my tea-making ritual.

I discovered that immersing myself in the steps for making a cup of tea calms me. It allows me to step away from the demands of my world and relax into the soothing, sure steps needed to make my tea. It allows me to be present in the moment. The tea-making ritual also connects me to the stories and legends of those who make the specialty teaware and the farmers who carefully tend the tea plants. It also connects us to those we choose to share our ritual with. In some ways, it goes deeper than simply a cup of tea.

This book is my way of paying tribute to the unique and compelling role tea has played, not only in my life but in traditions and countries worldwide. It is no in-depth analysis of tea, but for tea lovers and beginners, I hope it can guide you as you begin your tea adventure.

A BRIEF HISTORY OF TEA

Tea is a time-honored tradition in many cultures worldwide. Its history reaches over centuries, finding its origins in 2737 B.C.E. As the story goes, the Chinese Emperor Shen Nung was very particular about his health and personal well-being. He liked everything around him to be clean, and he only drank water that had been boiled to remove any impurities. As an herbalist, he was very familiar with the properties of many native plants and herbs.

One day, as Shen Nung was preparing his water to drink, the leaves of a nearby tea plant floated into his water. The hot water unintentionally brewed the tea leaves and turned the water slightly brown. The emperor drank the mixture and found that it invigorated him and kept him alert for his many meetings. And so tea as a drink was born.

The tea plant from which these leaves floated into the emperor's boiling water is the *Camellia sinensis* plant. All true teas come from this plant. The true teas are black, green, white, pu-erh, and oolong. Each tea is made by processing the leaves or buds of the tea plant. The degree of processing will determine the type of tea that is made.

Herbal infusions are not real teas but are, in fact, tisanes. They are not derived from the Camellia sinensis plant. They are made from the flowers, fruits, leaves, and bark of herbs and other plants. Despite not being a true tea, herbal infusions have created a niche for themselves in the tea market.

After the accidental discovery of tea by Shen Nung, tea was primarily used for medicinal purposes, but by the seventh century, tea had become a part of daily life in China. At this time, Buddhist monks from Japan began traveling to China. They returned home with the seeds of the tea plant, which started the spread of tea in Asia.

By the 10th century, tea had evolved into a highly coveted commodity, particularly along the Tea Horse Road between China and Tibet. This trading route was known for trading Chinese tea for Tibetan horses. In fact, on this route, tea bricks (compressed tea) were considered a form of currency used to pay for horses. Tea bricks were banned in the 1300s by the Ming dynasty, which led tea farmers and traders to find new ways of processing and transporting their tea. This ban on compressed tea led to the creation of what we now know as loose-leaf tea.

Tea came to Europe when trade with China opened up in the 1600s. The first shipment of tea came from China to Amsterdam in 1610 through the Dutch East

India Company and quickly gained popularity. The French quickly took up drinking tea, especially with milk. Tea fell into disfavor only during the French Revolution because of its association with royalty.

Meanwhile, in England, tea was introduced in 1662 by Catherine of Braganza, the Portuguese wife of Charles II. Tea became fashionable among the ladies of the royal court and the upper classes of British society. The first tea house was opened in 1717 by Thomas Twining, which allowed English homemakers to make tea at home and host tea parties. The growth of tea's popularity threatened the government's income from alcohol since most people were now drinking tea instead of going to the pub. As a result, the government began to heavily tax tea which led to black market smuggling and eventually resulted in the Boston Tea Party protest in the American colony, eventually leading up to the American War of Independence.

Britain was importing large amounts of tea from China to manage its local demand for the commodity but had fewer and fewer ways of paying for the tea because there was nothing China wanted to trade. Their attempt to interfere in the market with taxation ended badly, and they were running out of options. Britain needed to find a commodity that China would be willing to trade for, they came up with opium.

While the British fought with China over the trade in tea and opium, the British East India Company sought an alternative tea supplier to meet their demands and ensure no further disruptions to their supply. Fortuitously for the British, the state of Assam had an indigenous version of the tea plant known as *Camellia sinensis assamica* growing wild throughout the region.

The British saw this as an opportunity to extend their reach in India and cleared away forests to make way for tea plantations. India is now one of the largest producers of tea and one of the greatest tea consumers, averaging about 600 million cups a day (Lotusier, n.d.).

By this time, tea's popularity had grown not only in Europe but in the West as well. Americans were consuming large amounts of tea. In 1908, a tea merchant, Thomas Sullivan, inadvertently invented the first tea bag when he was looking for a way to send samples of his tea to his customers. He placed the loose tea leaves in small silk pouches. When the customers received the pouches, they added the whole bag to water, and so the tea bag was created. Today, over 159 million Americans drink tea daily (Tea Association of the U.S.A. Inc., 2022).

YOUR TEA TASTING STARTS HERE

The taste of tea is as unique and as varied as its history. The flavor and aroma of true teas can vary based on the climate, temperature, soil, and region in which the tea has been cultivated. It also depends heavily on how the tea leaves are harvested and processed. In much the same way, each cup of tea will be unique and should be based on your preferences.

The chapters in this book continue my adventure with tea. I love that tea has so many stories and legends surrounding it; each one is as special as the tea itself. Knowing and sharing these tales makes making and drinking a cup of tea even more extraordinary.

This adventure begins with understanding how to prepare that perfect cup of tea—from choosing the leaves to heating the water, they all come together to create that warm cup of goodness. I'll share the various methods you can use to brew your tea and some of my favorite tea tools I collected along the way.

Each type of tea has instructions for water temperature and brewing times that will help bring out the flavor profile and aroma in each of them. It is important to remember that these brewing tea recipes are flexible. Your tea should reflect your needs, so change it if necessary.

Once you've had a chance to learn about brewing each type of tea, I've created a chapter that is all about experimenting with your own tea blends. This chapter was a delightful (sometimes messy) experience. There is nothing quite like making your own tea blend. It's like creating a scent that is just you, except you can drink it! Tea blending is an excellent opportunity to carve some time out of your busy day to do something fun and creative. It's a great way to release anxiety and stress, resulting in an amazing cup of tea.

And finally, no tea drinker worth their salt would pass up an opportunity to try a cocktail with some of their favorite tea blends. All the cocktail recipes are relatively simple and don't require too many ingredients. Most of them you should have on hand, especially if you're blending your own teas. But before we can get to those party cocktails, we've got to get the basics covered. So let's get this adventure started with the perfect cup of tea.

1

THE FUNDAMENTALS OF TEA MAKING

Life can become overwhelming in a world where we are constantly bombarded with visual and auditory stimuli, making us search for ways to manage and cope with the daily stresses of our lives. It is in these moments that we seek relief through self-care rituals. We may find ourselves reaching for that warm cup of tea at these times.

Nothing eases the mind, soothes the soul, and energizes the body like a freshly brewed cup of tea. It's like a warm hug on a cold, dreary afternoon. Tea has been used for thousands of years as an alternative medicine to help heal the body, mind, and spirit.

The ancient Chinese used tea for its antibacterial, anti-inflammatory, and antioxidant properties to help maintain healthy bodies, aid in healing weakened bodies, and boost the body's natural immune system. Tea has also been known to reduce stomach cramps and aid with digestive issues. Certain teas can reduce menstrual cramps and can cleanse the digestive tract. Most importantly, a cup of tea can ease your stress and anxiety.

The simple act of preparing a cup of tea helps to focus the mind on the task at hand. As you make your tea, you concentrate on selecting your tea based on your mood, preparing the water, then pour the hot water into your cup. You then patiently wait for your tea to steep, and as you pick up that cup, the warmth spreads from your hands to your entire body, relaxing your muscles and relieving you of your tension. As you inhale the sweet aroma of that fresh cup of tea, your mind stills and focuses on the sensations associated with that cup of tea. In those moments, you are relieved of the hustle and bustle of your life. The process of making that cup of tea is an act of self-care. It does not need to be complicated; the pleasure is in simplicity.

BREWING THE PERFECT CUP OF TEA

Brewing a cup of tea should be a time of peace and focus. It is a moment in which you can escape from the demands of your daily life and give your mind a break. Believe it or not, this small break can improve productivity, increase concentration, and boost creativity. So do yourself a favor and make yourself that perfect cup of tea. It's nothing fancy and doesn't require an elaborate ceremony. A few simple steps will give you a cup of tea that will make a world of difference.

When making your tea, here are a few things you should consider:

1. Choose whole loose-leaf tea.

The taste and quality of your tea will depend on the type of tea you select. Try to pick whole-leaf teas that are of a single origin. This way, you can ensure some consistency. The tea in tea bags tends to be the leaves left over from the tea harvest and are usually of lower quality. The more you know about your tea, the higher the chances it will be of excellent quality.

2. Pay attention to the quality of your water.

Your tea is mainly made up of water, so it stands to reason that if the quality of your water is poor, then the taste of your tea will be equally poor. Bottled water is best, but you can use filtered tap water. For the best results, ensure your water is cold before boiling, and never reuse water that has already been boiled. The oxygen level is lower in reboiled water and will affect the taste of your tea.

3. Water temperature is critical.

Using just boiled water will burn your tea leaves, leaving a less desirable taste. Once your water has boiled, leave it for a few minutes before pouring it over your tea. Depending on the type of tea you are using, you will have to adjust the temperature of your water. Black tea is steeped at a higher temperature than green and white teas.

4. Know the steeping time.

Different types of tea require different brewing times, so make sure you know how long your tea should be steeped. The correct brewing time can affect your tea taste, just like finding the right temperature. Tea brewed for too long will be astringent, while too short a brewing time will result in a lack of flavor.

5. Give your tea some space.

Tea leaves are usually rolled during the processing stage, so when hot water is poured over them, they begin to unfurl and release their flavor. The more space the leaves have to open, the more flavorful the tea will be. If the tea leaves are cramped, they will never fully release all their flavor.

6. Preheat your teaware.

You will have better-tasting tea if you warm the teaware you are using. You can heat your teaware by rinsing it in warm water before pouring it into it. Doing this helps to keep the tea at the desired temperature.

It is important to note that all these considerations are made assuming you will use quality, loose-leaf teas.

Additionally, loose-leaf teas can be steeped multiple times. Each time will result in a slightly different yet high-quality flavor. So don't throw away your leaves after just one use. Just ensure that you use fresh water with each brewing. Then sit back and enjoy your perfectly brewed cup of warmth.

TEA BREWING METHODS

How you make your cup of tea is as unique as you are and is based mainly on personal choice and preference. However, because tea is so deeply ingrained in many of the world's cultures, many traditions and rituals are associated with brewing tea based on the different regions and cultural preferences. Here, we will highlight a few of the more popular methods of brewing tea, but remember, there is no right or wrong way to make your cup of tea. Just do what works for you.

Western-Style Brewing

As the name suggests, this method of brewing tea was created in the West and is the most popular way of brewing tea on this side of the world. Place a small amount of tea leaves in a tea ball or strainer and put this in your tea mug. You then pour the hot water over the ball and allow the tea to steep for about three minutes, after which you remove the tea ball and enjoy your tea. The most common version of this is the tea bag. This method is quick and easy and doesn't require many things.

Gong Fu Cha Brewing

This method is the traditional Chinese tea ceremony. It literally means "making tea with skill." You will require a proper tea set with various utensils to prepare your tea using this method. Unlike the Western style, in gong fu cha brewing, you use a large amount of tea leaves in a small pot of tea, and you brew the leaves for about 10 seconds. The tea is drunk from small cups. In this method, the tea leaves are usually infused multiple times.

Grandpa Style

This method may not be for everyone, but it's definitely a quick and easy way to brew your tea. You add your tea leaves directly to your mug, then pour your hot water over the leaves. Allow the leaves to brew for the requisite time, and then you can enjoy your mug of tea. As the tea leaves unfurl and absorb the water, they will sink to the bottom of the cup so you can enjoy your tea without worrying about drinking the leaves. Never drain your cup of tea to ensure you don't accidentally consume any leaves. Add more hot water to your cup when you are near the bottom, and allow the leaves to steep again for another cup of tea.

Boiling Method

This is one of the oldest methods of brewing tea. As the tea culture grew in ancient China, people boiled their tea leaves for extended periods to extract the most flavor. Tea boiling could sometimes last up to three hours, but not all tea leaves can withstand boiling water. Pu-erh and white tea leaves are better suited for boiling than black and green leaves. The latter leaves become too astringent when brewed for long periods. The tea leaves can also be boiled with different herbs and spices to create unique flavors and aromas. Boiled tea tastes best after about an hour of boiling. This method requires time and patience and is usually a ceremony in its own right.

Cold Brew

Cold brewing tea is a slow, almost delicate process that requires you to steep the tea in cold water for hours, even overnight, to extract the leaves' flavors. Because the tea is brewed in cold water, the caffeine content of the tea tends to be less since cold water does not extract as much caffeine from the leaves as hot water. The result is a smoother, sweeter tea since the cold water does not extract the tannins from the tea. To make cold brew tea, place the tea leaves in a pitcher and pour cold water over the leaves. Place the pitcher in the refrigerator overnight, and then enjoy your cold brew tea the following day. You can sweeten your tea with the sweetener of your choice. This option is excellent for hot, humid days but requires patience before enjoying the final product.

Whichever method you choose, make sure you use high-quality tea. It makes all the difference. Feel free to experiment to find what works best for you and fits your lifestyle. Remember, it will only be satisfying if it's personal to you.

TOOLS FOR MAKING THE PERFECT BREW

Tea brewing is a serious business; you need the right tools to make that perfect cup of tea. The marketplace is flooded with many gadgets to make brewing your tea easier and more fun. Your brewing method will be your primary determinant for the tools you need to make your tea. Because of its prevalence in various cultures and regions, tea-making tools will vary from place to place. Sometimes it can be overwhelming, and only some tools are necessary. This section will examine the essential equipment you need to make brewing your tea a relaxing and rewarding experience.

1. Electric Kettle

One of the great conveniences of the modern age, the electric kettle makes it quick and easy to boil water. Some electric kettles even offer you the option to set the temperature you want the water to get to, so it takes the guesswork out of finding the right temperature for your tea.

2. Tea Canisters

These are critical for storing your loose-leaf teas. The canisters should seal well and be airtight to prevent the tea leaves from absorbing other scents in the same space. These canisters also protect your leaves from absorbing moisture and degrading. Loose-leaf tea does not necessarily have an expiration date, but if it is not stored correctly, it can lose its flavor.

3. Tea Strainer

A tea strainer is useful, particularly if you're brewing your tea directly in your teapot. It prevents the tea leaves from getting into your cup when you pour the tea. Some tea strainers can double as tea infusers and remain in the pot while brewing.

4. Tea Infusers

An infuser is a fantastic option for brewing your tea. It gives your tea leaves the space needed to unfurl while keeping the leaves from getting into the water. It's also great because you can reuse the same leaves in another pot of tea without fuss.

5. Matcha Whisk and Scoop

If you're a fan of matcha, then this is a must-have! Matcha is usually prepared in a small bowl and whisked to create the frothiness associated with matcha. Find a whisk with a holder, which helps ensure it keeps its shape. The scoop is the ideal measure for your matcha powder to make the perfect cup of tea every time.

6. Milk Frother

If you love matcha or chai lattes, a milk frother will be one of your go-to tools. The milk frother will give you that creamy, frothy layer that is part of any good latte.

7. Tea Mugs

An essential part of making a cup of tea is the visual experience. A good set of tea mugs can make all the difference.

8. Cold Brewing Glass Bottle

If you love your cold brews, a cold brew bottle is essential. Opt for one with a built-in strainer, so you don't have to worry about any leaves in your drink. All you have to do is put your leaves and water in the bottle and place it in the fridge the night before. It's ready to go when you are the next day.

So you've bought your favorite tea leaves and made sure you've stocked up on all the essentials for making your own perfect cup of tea. It's time to discover some new and amazing recipes to incorporate into your teatime and self-care rituals.

2

DELICIOUS BLACK TEA EVERY TIME

Kenya is, in fact, the world's largest exporter of black tea. Although China and India both produce more tea than Kenya, more than half the tea is consumed domestically. Kenya exports, on average, about 300,000 tons of tea annually (Farrer's, 2020).

Black tea comes from the *Camellia sinensis sinensis* and the *Camellia sinensis assamica* plants. The former is native to the regions of China, while the latter is found in the countries of South Asia, including India and Sri Lanka. Black tea leaves are 100% oxidized, which gives them their black color. The black tea from the *assamica* variety has a higher caffeine content, but the amount of caffeine in an individual cup of tea depends on how long the tea is steeped.

In the United States, about 84% of all tea consumed is black, and most is consumed cold or iced (Tea Association of the U.S.A. Inc., 2022). The invention of tea bags in the 20th century made black tea a popular choice for most households and continues to be a pantry staple.

There are wide varieties of black teas, and most are named for the region in which they are produced. Chinese black teas include Lapsang souchong, Keemun, and congou. Indian black teas include Assam and Darjeeling, and Sri Lankan makes Ceylon black tea.

In this chapter, we will be exploring a variety of recipes using various black teas from around the world. You will be given step-by-step instructions and simple techniques for making delicious blends of black tea. Each recipe is a guide, but with time you can make them your own.

ASSAM BLACK TEA

Assam tea has a golden color and a strong, somewhat malty flavor. This unique flavor profile is attributed to the hot, humid region of India in which it is grown. This tea is delicious hot or cold.

Hot Assam Black Tea

Servings: 1

Steep Time: 5 minutes

Ingredients:

- 1 ½ tsp loose-leaf Assam tea
- 8 oz water, plus more for the teapot

Directions:

1. Place the water in an electric kettle and boil until it reaches 208 °F.

2. Pour some of the water into the teapot and swirl it around to warm up the teapot. Once the teapot is warm, discard the water.
3. Add the Assam tea leaves to the teapot, then pour the hot water over the leaves.
4. Cover the teapot and allow the tea to steep for 5 minutes.
5. Once steeped, strain the leaves and pour the tea into your teacup.
6. Add any sweetener of your choice and enjoy it warm.

Assam Cold Brew

Servings: 2

Steep Time: 5 minutes

Ingredients:

- 2 cups filtered water
- 2 ¼ tsp Assam loose-leaf tea
- 1 ½ tsp fresh lemon juice
- sugar to taste

Directions:

1. Place the water in a saucepan over medium-high heat and bring it to a boil.
2. Add the tea leaves and let it brew for 5 minutes, then remove the pan from the heat.
3. Strain the liquid into a jug and allow the brewed tea to cool.
4. Once the tea is cool, add the lemon juice and sugar, if using, and mix well.
5. Place the tea in the fridge and let it chill before enjoying it cold.

Assam Milk Tea

Servings: 1

Prep Time: 5 minutes

Cook Time: 8 minutes

Ingredients:

- ¼ cup tapioca pearls, quick cooking
- ½ cup water
- 1 tsp Assam loose-leaf tea
- ½ cup whole milk
- 2 tbsp simple syrup
- ice

Directions:

1. Prepare the tapioca pearls according to the package directions and set aside to cool.
2. Place the water in a small saucepan over medium heat and bring it to a boil. Once the water has reached a boil, turn off the heat and add the tea leaves to the hot water.
3. Allow the leaves to steep for at least 5 minutes. Let the tea cool completely.
4. Add the milk, simple syrup, and ice to a shaker. Carefully strain the cooled tea into the milk mixture. Shake well to combine the ingredients.
5. Add the tapioca pearls to a serving glass and add more ice, then carefully pour the milk tea over the pearls and ice.
6. Enjoy your chilled milk tea.

Spiced Assam Tea

Servings: 1

Prep Time: 5 minutes

Cook Time: 10 minutes

Ingredients:

- 2 cardamom pods
- 1 stick cinnamon
- 1 star anise
- sliced ginger
- 2 clove grains
- 1 tbsp Assam tea leaves
- ¾ cup water
- ½ cup whole milk
- sugar to taste

Directions:

1. Place all the spices except the ginger in a mortar and crush them with the pestle. This will help to release the flavors of the spices.
2. In a saucepan over medium heat, add the water, ginger, crushed spices, and tea leaves.
3. Allow the mixture to come to a boil, stirring frequently.
4. Once the mixture is boiling, add the milk and sugar and stir well.
5. Let the mixture boil for another 2 minutes.
6. The tea is ready when the mixture turns from a milky color to a light brown shade.

7. Once the tea is ready, remove the pan from the heat and strain the liquid into a teapot.
8. Enjoy your Assam milk tea warm. To make more, you can simply double the recipe.

CEYLON BLACK TEA

Ceylon tea is grown in the mountainous regions of Sri Lanka. The region has low temperatures, plentiful rainfall, and high humidity, making it an ideal place for tea plantations. Ceylon tea has a bold, citrusy flavor profile.

Warm Ceylon Black Tea

Servings: 1

Steep Time: 3 minutes

Ingredients:

- 1 tsp Ceylon loose-leaf tea
- 8 oz water plus extra

Directions:

1. Place the water in an electric kettle and boil to 200 °F.

2. Pour some of the water into the teapot and cups and swirl it around to warm up the teaware. Once they are warm, discard the water.
3. Add the Ceylon tea leaves to the teapot, then pour the hot water over the leaves.
4. Cover the teapot and allow the tea to steep for 3 minutes.
5. Once steeped, strain the leaves and pour the tea into your teacup.
6. Add any sweetener of your choice and enjoy it warm.

DARJEELING BLACK TEA

Darjeeling, as the name suggests, is grown in the tea estate of Darjeeling in Northern India. Darjeeling teas have a fruity or sometimes floral aroma and an almost spicy flavor profile. It is known as the "champagne of teas."

Darjeeling Iced Tea

Servings: 1

Steep Time: 5 minutes

Ingredients:

- 8 oz water
- 2 tsp Darjeeling loose-leaf tea
- 1 tbsp honey or maple syrup
- 2–3 orange slices
- ice
- mint leaves, optional

Directions:

1. Boil the water to 200 °F. Add the tea leaves to a cup, then pour the hot water over it. Allow the leaves to steep for 5 minutes.
2. Carefully strain the steeped tea into another glass.
3. While the tea is still warm, add the honey or maple syrup, as well as the orange slices. Squeeze the orange slices gently before adding them to the tea to release the juice.
4. Add ice to a tall glass, then pour the sweetened tea over the ice. Add the mint leaves if using,

and enjoy a refreshing glass of iced Darjeeling tea.

Darjeeling Sunburst Tea

Servings: 2

Cook Time: 5 minutes

Ingredients:

- 8 oz water
- 1 tsp ground turmeric
- 1 cup whole milk
- 1 tsp loose-leaf Darjeeling tea
- 1 cardamom pod
- 1 tsp honey

Directions:

1. Place water in a saucepan over medium heat and bring to a boil.
2. Once the water is boiling, add the turmeric, milk, and cardamom pod.
3. Add the tea leaves to the mixture and allow it to boil for another 2 minutes.

4. Once the tea is done, remove the saucepan from the heat and carefully strain the tea into two tea mugs.
5. Add honey as desired and serve warm.

Chamomile Darjeeling Tea

Servings: 1

Cook Time: 6 minutes

Ingredients:

- 1 tsp chamomile flowers, dried
- 8 oz water
- ½ tsp Darjeeling loose-leaf tea

Directions:

1. Bring the water to a boil in a kettle.
2. While the water is boiling, add the dried chamomile flowers to a teacup, then pour the hot water over the dried flowers. Allow the flowers to steep for about 1 minute.
3. Add the tea leaves to the cup and stir carefully. Let the tea brew for 5 minutes.
4. Carefully strain the tea leaves and enjoy your tea warm.

Darjeeling Iced Tea Latte

Servings: 2

Cook Time: 7 minutes

Ingredients:

- 1 cup water
- 1 tsp ginger powder
- ½ tsp cinnamon
- 4 tbsp sugar
- 2 tsp loose-leaf Darjeeling tea
- 5 oz whole milk, cold
- ice

Directions:

1. Bring the water to a boil in a saucepan over medium heat.
2. Reduce the pan to a simmer and add the ginger, cinnamon, sugar, and tea. Mix well, then cover the pan and allow the tea to brew for 5 minutes.
3. Once done, uncover the pan and carefully strain the tea into a large cup. Allow the tea to cool completely.
4. While the tea is cooling, use a milk frother to make the cold milk frothy.

5. Fill two glasses with ice, pour the cooled tea over the ice, then add the milk.
6. You can sprinkle some cinnamon powder over the milk.
7. Stir the tea before drinking and enjoy cold.

EARL GREY TEA

This tea got its name from Charles Grey, the second Earl of Grey, in the 19th century when he received this tea as a gift. The tea is usually a blend of Assam or Ceylon black tea with the oil of bergamot oranges added to it. This blend gives Earl Grey tea its unique citrusy flavor, making it one of the most popular tea blends worldwide.

Perfect Earl Grey Tea

Servings: 1

Steep Time: 5 minutes

Ingredients:

- 8 oz water, filtered if possible
- 1 tsp Earl Grey tea leaves (add ½ tsp more for a stronger tea)

Directions:

1. Place the water in an electric kettle and boil to 208 °F.
2. Pour some of the water into the teapot and cups and swirl it around to warm up the teaware. Once they are warm, discard the water.
3. Add the Earl Grey tea leaves to the teapot, then pour the hot water over the leaves.
4. Cover the teapot and allow the tea to steep for 3–5 minutes.
5. Once steeped, strain the leaves and pour the tea into your teacup.
6. You can add your choice of sweetener if desired. Earl Grey tea is traditionally served with a squeeze of lemon to enhance the citrusy flavor, but many in the United States add milk.

ENGLISH BREAKFAST TEA

English Breakfast is a blend of three black tea types: Assam, Ceylon, and Darjeeling. This blend makes it a strong, robust tea perfect for mornings or early afternoon boosts. English Breakfast tea pairs perfectly with honey, brown or white sugar, maple syrup, agave, cinnamon, and cardamom. For a fruity profile, you can try brewing your leaves with mango, coconut, peaches, or strawberries. You can steep the blend with dried rose or jasmine flowers to make the blend a little lighter.

Classic English Breakfast Tea

Servings: 1

Steep Time: 3–5 minutes

Ingredients:

- 8 oz water
- 1 tsp English breakfast tea leaves
- 1 tsp sugar
- 1 tsp milk

Directions:

1. In a kettle, boil the water. While the water is boiling, add the tea leaves to your teapot.
2. Once the water is ready, pour it over the tea leaves and cover the teapot.
3. Allow the tea to steep for 3 minutes. If you like your tea stronger, leave it for 5 minutes.
4. Carefully strain the tea into a teacup.
5. Add the sugar and milk and mix well.
6. Enjoy your tea warm. Remember, you can use the same leaves for another cup of tea.

IRISH BREAKFAST TEA

Irish breakfast tea is made mainly with Assam black tea, which gives it a bold, robust, malty flavor profile. In some instances, it may contain a mix of black teas. It is quite strong with a high caffeine content making it an ideal morning drink to start your day. For the most part, Irish breakfast is taken with milk and sugar and is meant to be part of a hearty breakfast. Because of its robust flavor, Irish breakfast tea pairs well with strong cheeses, steak, roast beef, bacon, chocolate, carrot cake, and fruit salads.

Traditional Irish Breakfast Brew

Servings: 2

Steep Time: 4 minutes

Ingredients:

- 8 oz hot water
- 1 tsp Irish breakfast tea leaves
- 1 ½ oz Irish whiskey
- 1 tsp sugar
- milk, to taste

Directions:

1. Place the Irish breakfast tea leaves in a cup and pour the hot water over the leaves. Allow the tea to steep for 4 minutes.
2. Carefully strain the brewed tea into a larger cup, then add the sugar and mix until the sugar dissolves.
3. Add the whiskey and milk and stir well to combine.
4. Enjoy your tea warm.

Irish Breakfast Iced Tea

Servings: 12

Prep Time: 5 minutes

Cook Time: 5 minutes

Ingredients:

- 12 cups cold water, filtered if possible
- 12 Irish breakfast tea bags
- 24 cubes frozen lemonade, sweetened

Directions:

1. In a saucepan, add the water and let it come to a boil, then remove the pan from the heat.
2. Add the tea bags to the hot water and allow the tea to steep for 5 minutes, then remove the tea bags.
3. Let the brewed tea cool completely, then transfer it to a pitcher.
4. To serve, place two ice cubes in a glass and pour the brewed tea over the cubes.
5. Stir and enjoy!

KEEMUN BLACK TEA

Keemun black tea is also known as Keemun Gongfu and is one of China's most popular black teas. This tea was first produced in 1875 in the Chinese province of Anhui. It is the only black tea on China's list of top 10 teas. It is considered to be a high-quality tea with a mellow flavor and the aroma of springtime. When brewed, the color of the tea can range from bright oranges to red.

Classic Keemun Black Tea

Servings: 1

Steep Time: 2–3 minutes

Ingredients:

- 8 oz water
- 1 tsp Keemun tea leaves

Directions:

1. Place the water in an electric kettle and boil to 194 °F.
2. Pour some of the water into the teacup and swirl it around to warm up the cup. Once it is warm, discard the water.
3. Place the Keemun leaves in a tea infuser and place the infuser in your cup.
4. Pour the hot water over the leaves and allow the tea to steep for 2–3 minutes.
5. Once steeped, remove the infuser and enjoy your cup of tea.
6. You can add any sweetener of your choice as well as milk. Avoid adding lemon to Keemun tea because the acidity of the lemon will give the tea a very tart taste.

KENYAN BLACK TEA

Tea was first brought to Kenya in the early 1900s by colonial settlers, and its tropical climate, with long, sunny days and adequate rainfall, makes it ideal as a tea-growing region. Although Kenya began cultivating tea later than its Asian counterparts, it has made a global name for itself as the world's top exporter of black tea and the third-largest producer of black tea. Kenyan black tea is used as the base of many tea blends throughout the world.

Kenyan Ginger Tea

Servings: 4

Prep Time: 10 minutes

Cook Time: 5 minutes

Ingredients:

- 2 cups water
- ¼ cup white sugar
- 1 cinnamon stick
- 4 cloves, crushed
- 1 tsp fresh ginger, crushed
- 4 green cardamom pods, crushed
- 2 tbsp Kenyan loose-leaf tea

- 2 cups whole milk

Directions:

1. Add the water to a medium saucepan and bring it to a boil over high heat.
2. Once the water is boiling, reduce the heat to low and add the sugar, cinnamon, cloves, ginger, cardamom, and tea leaves. Mix well to combine.
3. Allow the mixture to simmer for 3 minutes, stirring from time to time.
4. After 3 minutes, add the milk and mix well.
5. Let this simmer for another 2 minutes, then remove the pan from the heat.
6. Carefully strain the tea into four cups and serve warm.

LAPSANG SOUCHONG

Lapsang souchong is a special oxidized black tea grown in the mountains of the Fujian province of China. As the story goes, it was made by accident by farmers fleeing from soldiers. In their haste to escape, the farmers quickly dried the tea leaves over a fire and buried the sacks of dried tea to ensure they did not spoil. The buried tea was eventually sold to the Dutch, who loved the smoky tea and requested more.

Lapsang souchong is a full-bodied tea with a smoky flavor and a bacon-like aroma. It is not as bitter as other black teas and is usually brewed strong and taken without any sweetener.

Lapsang Souchong Tea

Servings: 1

Steep Time: 5 minutes

Ingredients:

- 8 oz water, plus a little extra
- 1 tsp Lapsang souchong tea leaves
- sweetener of choice, optional (note that honey may alter the flavor profile of the tea while maple syrup can enhance the natural smoky flavors)

Directions:

1. Place the water in an electric kettle and boil to 208 °F.
2. Pour some of the hot water into the teapot and cups and swirl it around to warm up the

teaware. Once they are warm, discard the water.

3. Add the Lapsang souchong tea leaves to the teapot, then pour the hot water over the leaves.
4. Cover the teapot and allow the tea to steep for 5 minutes.
5. Once steeped, strain the leaves and pour the tea into your teacup.
6. Add any sweetener of your choice and enjoy it warm.

MASALA CHAI

Legend has it that a form of masala chai was drunk 5,000 years ago in the royal courts of India. The rulers then mixed various spices and drank them to stay alert during court sessions. Of course, there were no tea leaves, so the drink was completely caffeine-free.

In the 19th century, the British discovered the tea plant growing wild in Assam and began to set up tea farms to cultivate tea and reduce its dependency on Chinese tea, with whom it was currently at odds. Most of the tea produced in India then was exported, and any tea left in the domestic market was too expensive for the general populace to afford.

Instead, tea sellers began to brew the leftover tea leaves with milk, spices, and sugar to create an intensely flavored brew that was cheap. And so, masala chai became a drink of the general population. It has since grown to become one of the most popular forms of tea consumed across the globe and remains a staple of Indian life. Each region of India has its variation that is uniquely theirs.

Traditional Masala Chai

Servings: 2

Prep Time: 5 minutes

Cook Time: 15 minutes

Ingredients:

- 1 cup water
- 3 cloves, whole
- 5 black peppercorns
- 1 star anise
- 5 green cardamom pods
- ½ cinnamon stick
- 2 slices ginger
- 2 tbsp loose-leaf black tea (Assam, Darjeeling, or any you prefer)
- 1 cup milk

- 2 tsp sweetener of your choice

Directions:

1. Add the water to a medium saucepan over high heat and bring to a boil.
2. While the water is boiling, add the cloves, peppercorns, star anise, and cardamom to a mortar and crush the spices together with the pestle.
3. Add the crushed spices to the boiling water, then add the ginger and muddle it in the pot.
4. Add the cinnamon to the water and bring the mixture to a simmer, then lower the heat and let it simmer for about 8 minutes. Turn off the heat.
5. Add the tea leaves to the mixture and allow it to steep for 5 minutes.
6. Turn the heat back on and add the milk. Stir well and let it come to a simmer again, then remove the pan from the heat.
7. Add the sweetener of your choice to the tea and stir well.
8. Carefully strain into two mugs and serve warm.

YUNNAN BLACK TEA

As the name suggests, Yunnan black tea is produced in the Yunnan province in south China. Yunnan is said to be the birthplace of tea because history has it that the leaf from a tea tree accidentally fell into the cup of hot water of the Chinese emperor in 2700 B.C.E. The leaf turned the water brown just before the emperor drank it, and it is said that he found it energizing and requested that this drink always be made for him.

Yunnan tea is a fully oxidized black tea grown in the mountainous regions of the province. The high elevation and mild climate allow the tea plants a long growing season. Although it is a black tea, when steeped, the Yunnan tea has a golden yellow color and a milder, sweeter taste than most black teas.

Classic Yunnan Black Tea

Servings: 1

Steep Time: 3 minutes

Ingredients:

- 8 oz water, plus more
- 1 tsp Yunnan black tea leaves
- milk, optional

Directions:

1. Place the water in an electric kettle and boil to 208 °F.
2. Pour some of the water into the teapot and cups and swirl it around to warm up the teaware. Once they are warm, discard the water.
3. Add the Yunnan tea leaves to the teapot, then pour the hot water over the leaves.
4. Cover the teapot and allow the tea to steep for 3 minutes.
5. Once steeped, strain the leaves and pour the tea into your teacup.
6. Add milk if you choose to, and enjoy it warm.

Black tea continues to be the most popular type of tea consumed globally. Over the years and particularly during the pandemic, tea drinkers have become more discerning about their tea and have begun experimenting with and trying other types of tea. The next chapter explores the world of green tea. For many, it is an acquired taste, but as we journey through the various green teas, perhaps you can find one you enjoy.

3

BEAT THE BITTERNESS—HOW TO BREW THE PERFECT CUP OF GREEN TEA

The tea that the Chinese emperor accidentally discovered in 2700 B.C.E. was, in fact, green tea, but until the 14th century, green tea was costly. The upper classes in Chinese society could only enjoy it. Only during the 14th century did green tea become more accessible to the general population as a drink for enjoyment and medicinal purposes.

Green tea made its way to the West in the 19th century as more and more European explorers journeyed East and back. It became so popular in England that it became a national beverage. England remains one of the largest tea importers, and China remains the world's top tea producer.

Green tea is known for its health and wellness benefits primarily because it retains most of its nutritional value. This is because it does not undergo the oxidation process. The tea itself is mild, with an almost grassy taste. Most green teas are golden or yellow, while teas like the Japanese sencha have a bright green hue. The high flavonoid content in green tea helps to lower cholesterol and reduce blood clotting while boosting mental acuity.

BILUOCHUN

Biluochun literally means "green snail in spring." The tea gets its name because the dried leaves are tightly curled and silvery green giving them the appearance of snails. This tea is cultivated in the Jiangsu province of

China. It has a light, sweet, fruity taste and a floral aroma. Traditionally, Biluochun is brewed in a *gaiwan* or glass cup, but it can be brewed in a teapot or cup.

Classic Biluochun Tea

Servings: 1

Steep Time: 1–2 minutes

Ingredients:

- 8 oz water, plus more
- 1 tsp Biluochun tea leaves

Directions:

1. Place the water in an electric kettle and boil to 176 °F.
2. Pour some of the water into the teapot and cup and swirl it around to warm up the teaware. Once they are warm, discard the water.
3. Add the Biluochun tea leaves to the teapot, then pour the hot water over the leaves.
4. Cover the teapot and allow the tea to steep for 1–2 minutes.
5. Once steeped, strain the leaves and pour the tea into your teacup.

GENMAICHA

Genmaicha, or "brown rice tea," is a Japanese green tea. It gets its name because the leaves are mixed with roasted brown rice kernels. The rice gives the tea its signature warm, toasty aroma and flavor. When brewed, the tea is pale yellow and very mild. It has a grassy taste and is slightly sweet.

Genmaicha Brew

Servings: 1

Steep Time: 30 seconds

Ingredients:

- 8 oz water, plus more
- 1 tsp genmaicha tea leaves

Directions:

1. Place the water in an electric kettle and boil to 208 °F.
2. Pour some of the water into the teapot and cup and swirl it around to warm up the teaware. Once they are warm, discard the water.

3. Add the genmaicha tea leaves to the teapot, then pour the hot water over the leaves.
4. Cover the teapot and allow the tea to steep for just 30 seconds. If you leave it longer, your tea will be bitter.
5. Once steeped, strain the leaves and pour the tea into your teacup.
6. You can steep the leaves in hot water again but don't leave the leaves to steep. Pour the tea into the cup straightaway after the second infusion. The tea leaves have already been opened with the first infusion, so there is no need to wait for the tea to steep.

GYOKURO

Gyokuro is probably the most expensive of the Japanese green teas. It is a high-quality green tea with a distinct *umami* flavoring. The taste of this green tea results from the high amount of the amino acid, L-theanine, found in the tea. During processing, this tea is shaded from the sun for a number of days before harvesting. As a result, the L-theanine is not converted to catechins, which gives the green tea its astringency.

Gyokuro is considered a luxury tea, even in Japan, and is brewed carefully and served in small cups. The key to brewing gyokuro is to ensure that you get the right water temperature to bring out the sweetness of the tea. Specific tea sets are used for brewing gyokuro called kyusu, but you can use a regular tea mug.

Traditional Gyokuro Tea

Servings: 2

Steep Time: 2 ½ minutes

Ingredients:

- 4 oz water
- 3 tbsp gyokuro tea leaves

Directions:

1. In a kettle, boil the water to 140 °F. If the water is too hot, the tea will become extremely astringent, and you will destroy the gyokuro tea leaves.
2. Place the tea leaves in a small teapot and carefully pour the water.
3. Allow the tea to steep for 2 ½ minutes. Steeping the tea for this period of time enhances the thick creaminess of the tea. This green tea takes longer to steep because the water is relatively cooler than that used in other teas.

4. Carefully strain the tea into the cups, alternating between each cup until all the tea is poured and there are equal amounts in each cup. Pouring in this manner increases the richness of the tea.
5. Serve immediately and drink in small sips to savor the tea's unique flavor and texture.

LAOSHAN

This green tea is grown in the Shandong province of China, famous for its green teas. Laoshan is one of the northernmost tea-cultivating regions in China, and as such, great care has to be taken to ensure that the tea plants are not affected by the frosts.

The leaves of the Laoshan tea are very tightly curled, making it an excellent tea for steeping repeatedly. The tea is nutty and sweet but still retains a grassy, slightly umami flavoring. When brewed, the tea has a pale yellow-green hue, almost like a pear.

Laoshan Tea

Servings: 1

Steep Time: 3 minutes

Ingredients:

- 1 cup water, plus more
- 1 tsp Laoshan tea leaves

Directions:

1. Place the water in an electric kettle and boil to 176 °F.
2. Pour some of the water into a small teapot and cup and swirl it around to warm up the teaware. Once they are warm, discard the water.
3. Add the Laoshan tea leaves to the teapot, then pour the hot water over the leaves.
4. Gently shake the teapot to ensure all the leaves are fully soaked, and allow the tea to steep for 3 minutes.
5. Once steeped, strain the leaves and pour the tea into your teacup.
6. You can re-steep the tea up to three times.

DRAGON WELL

Dragon Well, or Longjing, tea is another of China's famous green teas. It is cultivated in Hangzhou in the Zhejiang province. The tea is easily recognized by its smooth, flattened leaves, which is done by shaping in a hot wok. The tea is normally harvested by hand to ensure that the tea leaves are uniform, which is crucial for producing the highest-grade tea. The tea has a sweet, nutty flavor and is mellow.

Dragon Well Tea

Servings: 1

Steep Time: 2–3 minutes

Ingredients:

- 8 oz water, plus extra
- 2 tsp Dragon Well tea leaves

Directions:

1. Heat the water to 176 °F.
2. Heat a glass teacup by adding some of the boiled water and swirling it around. Once the glass is warmed, discard the water.

3. In the glass, add about ¼ cup of the boiled water then add the Dragon Well tea leaves. Swirl the glass teacup gently, so all the leaves are soaked and sink to the bottom.
4. Add the rest of the water to fill the cup.
5. Wait for all the leaves to sink to the bottom of the cup before you begin drinking the tea. This should take about 2–3 minutes. If your leaves are not sinking, it means your water is not hot enough.
6. Drink your tea until there is about ¼ cup of liquid left then, you can pour more water for another infusion.

MATCHA

Probably one of the most famous Japanese green teas, matcha is made by grinding green tea leaves into a fine powder. It is the tea used in traditional Japanese tea ceremonies and usually requires a matcha bowl and whisk to prepare the tea.

Matcha is bright green and has a slightly bitter taste. It is said to be full of antioxidant goodness that can help reduce blood pressure and increase metabolism. In recent years, particularly in the United States, the consumption of matcha has increased because of its potential health benefits.

Like all teas, there are different grades of matcha. Ceremonial-grade matcha is the best tasting and has the most vibrant green hue. This also means that it's more expensive than the lower-quality grades. Opt for the ceremonial grade of matcha if you only drink your matcha tea with water. If you're making lattes and using it for cooking, you can use a lower-grade tea.

Matcha Brew

For this recipe, you will need a matcha bowl, a whisk, and a small sifter for the best results.

Servings: 1

Prep Time: 5 minutes

Ingredients:

- 8 oz water
- ¼ tsp matcha
- sweetener of choice, optional

Directions:

1. In an electric kettle, boil the water until it reaches 176 °F.
2. While the water is boiling, sift the matcha into your bowl to remove any clumps.

3. Add 2 oz of the hot water to the bowl with the matcha and whisk quickly in the shape of a "W." This will help to break up the matcha and produce a foamy layer on top.
4. Now pour in the remaining 6 oz of water and whisk again until you get that foamy layer.
5. Add your sweetener, if using, and enjoy straight from the bowl.
6. You can replace the 6 oz of water with steamed milk to create a creamy tea.

SENCHA

Sencha is another Japanese green tea quite popular worldwide and the most regularly consumed tea in Japan. It has a grassy, slightly sweet taste and, when brewed, is a pale yellow-green. To brew the perfect cup of sencha, you must pay careful attention to the temperature of your water. If it's too hot, then you will get bitter-tasting tea. Similarly, if you brew sencha too long, it will also be bitter.

To make sencha tea, the tea plant leaves are steamed, rolled, and dried, and then the whole dried leaves are infused in hot water. This process is what makes sencha tea leaves unique. A tea farmer, Nagatani Soen, created this method of steaming the leaves after they were dried. He discovered that by preparing the leaves in this manner, the flavor of the tea was preserved until they were immersed in hot water. Nagatani Soen is considered to be the father of modern Japanese tea, and a shrine is dedicated to him near his family home in Japan.

Sencha Tea

Servings: 1

Steep Time: 1–2 minutes

Ingredients:

- 4 oz water
- 1 tsp sencha tea leaves

Directions:

1. Place the water in an electric kettle and boil to 176 °F.
2. While the water is boiling, add the sencha tea leaves to the teapot.
3. Once the water comes to a boil, pour it into your teacup and allow the water to cool for about 2 minutes.
4. When the water cools down, add the water to the teapot with the tea leaves.

5. Allow the tea to steep for 1–2 minutes.
6. Once steeped, pour the tea into your teacup and enjoy.

Green tea can be an acquired taste and, if not appropriately brewed, can be bitter. But you shouldn't have to worry about that anymore because you're well on your way to becoming a green tea brewmaster. Now that you've gotten the hang of green teas, it's time to move on to the artisanal world of oolong teas.

4

HOW TO ENJOY YOUR OOLONG

If you're in the United States, chances are you're most accustomed to black tea, and while there's a growing appreciation for green teas, we haven't quite begun to explore the world of oolong teas. In most places, if you requested an oolong tea, you would probably be met with a blank stare simply because oolong teas are less common in the West than they are in Asia and other Eastern regions.

Oolong tea, however, has a long history in Asia and is the stuff around which legends have been made. In one such legend, there was a tea farmer named Sulong who lived in the Fujian province of China and spent his days outdoors, and because of this, he was deeply tanned. The villagers called him "Wulong" or "dark dragon." One spring day, Wulong went up the mountains to pluck tea leaves carrying his tea basket and a gun (he hoped to catch a wild animal for dinner). On his way back down the mountain after picking the tea leaves, he saw a mountain deer. He chased the deer for a long time before finally shooting and catching it.

By the time Wulong arrived home, it was early evening, and he and his family began preparing the meal, forgetting about the tea leaves. The leaves were left out all night, and the edges of the leaves had started to turn red. Wulong decided to process the leaves still, and much to his astonishment, the processed leaves were full of flavor and highly aromatic. The other village farmers began to process their leaves in much the same manner, producing semi-oxidized oolong tea.

Another story traces the origins of oolong tea to the Beiyuan tea, one of the earliest tribute teas in Fujian province. The Beiyuan area of Fujian province is said to have produced teas since the end of the Tang dynasty, around 900. It is believed that the tea god, Zhang Ting Hui, led the villagers of the areas to create tea plantations and produce the famous Beiyuan tea. In official records, the tea is described as sweet and smooth, and the process by which it was made is similar to that of oolong. As many tea experts consider such, Beiyuan tea to be the predecessor of oolong tea.

Oolong tea is a variety of tea that is somewhere between a black and green tea and requires the tea farmer to have great skill to perfect the right balance. Oolong teas offer a range of depth of flavor as well as complexity. Oolongs can range from floral to chocolatey to fruity or roasted. The possibilities for oolong teas are endless, and you will find far more diversity in these teas than in your black or green teas.

The quality of an oolong tea depends heavily on the person processing it. If one step is altered or missed, you can ruin an entire batch of tea. Oolongs are a partially oxidized tea, so careful attention must be paid to how long the tea leaves are allowed to oxidize after being plucked before the oxidation process is halted. Oolong teas are usually between 8 and 85% oxidized.

A tea as complex as an oolong requires some brewing skills, or you may ruin the hard work of the tea worker who painstakingly coaxed the flavors and aromas out of the leaves. In general, oolong tea is best enjoyed in small amounts to truly appreciate its complexity. Each infusion of an oolong tea produces a new subtle flavor so that with each infusion of the same leaves, you feel as if you're experiencing a whole new cup of tea. Additionally, oolong tea leaves are generally larger than green or black teas, so they need more space to open up and release their flavors.

BAI HAO OOLONG

Bai Hao oolong is one of the highest-quality oolong teas grown in the northwest region of Taiwan. Its name means white tip and refers to the small white buds picked with the tea plant's top two leaves during harvesting. The unique characteristics of the Bai Hao tea are a result of the humid, foggy climate of the region. Unlike most Taiwanese oolongs, which are harvested in the spring, Bai Hao oolong is picked in the summertime. The brewed tea is very smooth with a fruity flavor and a honeyed texture.

Bai Hao is also known as "Oriental Beauty," a name given to it after a British merchant, in the early 20th century, presented the tea to Queen Elizabeth II. The queen was so delighted by the delicate aroma and flavor of the tea that she named it "Oriental Beauty."

Bai Hao

Servings: 1

Steep Time: 3–4 minutes

Ingredients:

- 8 oz water plus extra, filtered
- 1 tsp Bai Hao tea leaves

Directions:

1. In an electric kettle, heat the water until it reaches 190 °F.
2. Pour some of the water into the teapot and cup and swirl it around to warm up the teaware. Once they are warm, discard the water.
3. Add the Bai Hao tea leaves to the teapot, then pour the hot water over the leaves.
4. Allow the tea to steep for 3–4 minutes.
5. Once steeped, strain the leaves and pour the tea into your teacup.
6. Enjoy your tea warm.

BAOZHONG OR POUCHONG

Baozhong was originally grown in Fujian province in China but was brought to Taiwan by the tea merchant Fu-Yuan Wu about 150 years ago. Today, Baozhong is produced in Taipei. Unlike other oolong teas, Baozhong has twisted tea leaves, which are less oxidized than most other oolong teas. As a result of its lower degree of oxidation, Baozhong often bears similar characteristics to green tea, but you can still tell the difference. Baozhong has large, bright leaves that are twisted and have more of a floral flavor than the grassy notes of green teas. There is no astringency in the brewed tea. It is a very fragrant tea that can be enjoyed on a regular basis.

Baozhong Tea

Servings: 1

Steep Time: 2 minutes

Ingredients:

- 8 oz water plus more, filtered
- 1 tsp Baozhong tea leaves

Directions:

1. Place the water in an electric kettle and boil to 194 °F.
2. Pour some of the water into the teapot and cup and swirl it around to warm up the teaware. Once they are warm, discard the water.
3. Add the Baozhong tea leaves to the teapot, then pour the hot water over the leaves.
4. Cover the teapot and allow the tea to steep for 2 minutes.
5. Once steeped, strain the leaves and pour the tea into your teacup.
6. For any additional infusions, increase the brewing time by 30 seconds.

DA HONG PAO

In English, Da Hong Pao translates to "big red robe." As the legend goes, in 1385, a scholar, Ju Zi Ding, was on his way to sit the imperial exam to advance his career as an official. On his way to his exam, he fell ill in Wuyishan and could not continue. Fortunately, a monk passed by and gave Ju Zi Ding a special tea with healing qualities. Soon after drinking the tea, he felt much better and could make it to the imperial exam on time.

He not only passed his exam but received the highest score and was awarded with an imperial scarlet robe.

Ju Zi Ding was extremely grateful to the monk who assisted him, so he returned to Wuyishan to thank him and inquire about the tea's origins. The monk showed him the tea bushes, and Ju Zi Ding immediately removed his red robe and wrapped it around it three times out of sincere gratitude. Since then, the tea has been called Da Hong Pao.

In 2002, 20 grams of Da Hong Pao tea leaves were sold at auction for $28,000, making it more expensive than gold. These leaves were harvested from what is considered the mother trees. Today, those mother trees are protected by armed guards, and no one is allowed to harvest leaves from these six remaining mother trees. The leaves from these trees are said to be kept for elite guests. But you can still get a good-quality cup of Da Hong Pao for much less.

This Chinese oolong is grown in the Wuyi Mountains in China. It is a very oxidized oolong which makes its leaves dark in appearance. Because it is considered a rock, it has a hint of mineral notes but a very sweet scent. It is considered to be a highly complex tea with layers of flavor.

Da Hong Pao

Servings: 1

Steep Time: 1 minute

Ingredients:

- 8 oz water plus more
- 1 ½ tsp Da Hong Pao tea leaves

Directions:

1. Place the water in an electric kettle and boil to 95–205 °F.
2. Pour some of the water into the teapot and cup and swirl it around to warm up the teaware. Once they are warm, discard the water.
3. Add the Da Hong Pao tea leaves to a tea strainer, then place them in your cup.
4. Pour the hot water over the leaves and allow the tea to steep for 1 minute.
5. Once steeped, remove the tea strainer and enjoy your cup of tea.
6. Da Hong Pao tea can be reinfused up to six times. For each additional infusion, add an extra minute to the steeping time.

FENG HUANG DAN CONG OOLONG

This is another famous Chinese oolong cultivated in the Phoenix Mountain in Guangdong, China. According to legend, during the Song dynasty (960–1279), the child emperor, Zhao Bing, fled to the Wu Dong Mountain during a war. The farmers in the region found the child, but he was severely dehydrated and bruised. They gave him the leaves of the tea bushes to chew, allowing him to regain enough strength to make it to the village for treatment. As a result of the miraculous recovery of the emperor, the Dan Cong tea was known as the "Tea of Song." Unfortunately, Zhao Bing did not survive the war and jumped into the sea at the age of eight, bringing with him the end of the Song dynasty. It was not until the Qing dynasty that Dan Cong tea would be rewarded for its unique qualities.

The Feng Huang Dan Cong oolong leaves are quite large and crinkled and dark brown with a hint of red. When brewed, the tea is golden and clear in color. The brewed tea has a peachy flavor and is highly fragrant.

Dan Cong Oolong Brew

Servings: 1

Steep Time: 20–30 seconds

Ingredients:

- 8 oz water plus more
- 1–1 ½ tsp Dan Cong tea leaves

Directions:

1. Place the water in an electric kettle and boil to 207 °F.
2. Pour some of the water into the teapot and cup and swirl it around to warm up the teaware. Once they are warm, discard the water.
3. Add the Dan Cong tea leaves to a tea strainer, then place it in your cup.
4. Pour the hot water over the leaves and allow the tea to steep for 20–30 seconds.
5. Once steeped, remove the tea strainer and enjoy your cup of tea.
6. This amount of Dan Cong tea leaves can be reinfused up to four times. Reduce the brewing time to under 20 seconds for each additional infusion, or the tea may become bitter.

TIE GUAN YIN

Tie Guan Yin, or the "Iron Goddess of Mercy" is a Chinese oolong grown in Anxi County in Fujian province. The leaves are shaped into small balls that are tightly rolled without any branches.

As the story goes, Tie Guan Yin was discovered during the Qing dynasty about 300 years ago. A poor farmer found an abandoned temple with a statue of Goddess Guan Yin. He spent the next few days cleaning and caring for the temple. One day, while asleep in the temple, the goddess appeared in his dreams and told him where he would find his reward for his service to her temple. It just so happens that the farmer was rewarded with a tea plant that he planted in his garden. This tea plant brought him success and wealth.

Tie Guan Yin can range in flavor and aroma because the leaves can be highly oxidized or less oxidized. Most of today's Tie Guan Yin teas have a bright yellow color and a floral aroma with a creamy, smooth texture. They can be roasted or unroasted. They can also be very green or very aged.

Tie Guan Yin Tea

Servings: 1

Steep Time: 1–2 minutes

Ingredients:

- 8 oz water plus more
- 1–1 ½ tsp Tie Guan Yin tea leaves

Directions:

1. Place the water in an electric kettle and boil to 194–207 °F.
2. Pour some of the water into the teapot and cup and swirl it around to warm up the teaware. Once they are warm, discard the water.
3. Add the Tie Guan Yin tea leaves to a tea strainer, then place it in your cup.
4. Pour the hot water over the leaves and allow the tea to steep for 2 minutes.
5. Once steeped, remove the tea strainer and enjoy your cup of tea.
6. You can re-steep this tea but reduce the steeping time to one minute since the leaves would have already unfurled.

TUNG TING

Tung Ting, or "Frozen Summit," is named after the mountain on which this tea is grown. Tung Ting is a Taiwanese oolong tea cultivated in Nantou County in central Taiwan. The tea plants were brought from the Wuyi Mountains in China to Taiwan about 150 years ago by Lin Feng Chi. Tung Ting is considered one of Taiwan's first teas.

Because Tung Ting is a high-mountain tea, it tends to have a floral aroma with a sweet aftertaste. When brewed, it is golden yellow with a mellow, fruity taste. The leaves are usually hand-rolled into tight balls, and the leaves are glossy, dark green.

Tung Ting Tea

Servings: 1

Steep Time: 40 seconds

Ingredients:

- 8 oz water plus more
- 1–2 tsp Tung Ting tea leaves

Directions:

1. Place the water in an electric kettle and boil to 190–200 °F.
2. Pour some water into the teacup and swirl it around to warm up the teaware. Once it is warm, discard the water.
3. Add the Tung Ting tea leaves to a tea strainer, then place it in your cup.
4. Pour the hot water over the leaves and allow the tea to brew for 40 seconds.
5. Once steeped, remove the tea strainer and enjoy your cup of tea.
6. You can re-steep this tea three times but increase the steeping time by five seconds for the second infusion and five more seconds for the third infusion. If you plan on reusing the leaves more than three times, you will need to add ten additional seconds for each infusion thereafter.

By now, you should have a good handle on brewing oolong teas; you may even be able to say you're an expert. Now is a good time to venture into the world of pu-erh teas. Pu-erh teas are particularly unique and require careful brewing to elicit just the right flavors and textures.

5

YOUR ULTIMATE GUIDE TO BREWING THE PERFECT PU-ERH TEA

Pu-erh tea has a long history dating back to the Yunnan province in China during the Han dynasty (25–220). Trade in pu-erh tea started during the Tang dynasty and reached the height of popularity during the Qing dynasty. The tea was traded along what was known as the Tea Horse Road. Long caravans of mules and horses transported the tea along this route.

The tea got its name from Pu-erh County, where the tea was traded. Tea merchants purchased the tea at this trading post and then hired caravans to carry it back to their hometowns or villages. These roads were extremely long, and it would take weeks for goods to be transported from one location to another. As such, the demand for tea that would not go bad and that could be transported easily increased.

This increasing demand led suppliers to find ways to lengthen the so-called "shelf life" of their teas. The tea merchants began packing their tea into bricks instead of leaving whole tea leaves. These compressed bricks were far easier to transport on a horse or mule's back over long distances and sometimes treacherous terrain. Sometimes, it could be months or years before the tea arrived at its final destination.

It was discovered that during these extended journeys, the tea changed color from green to amber and then to a dark tea. The taste of the tea also became smoother and fruitier, almost like a fine wine. These long months caused the tea to age and ferment, meaning that microbes caused changes to the tea's enzymes, leading to what is known today as pu-erh tea.

Pu-erh is a post-fermented tea, meaning that the tea goes through the fermentation process after the leaves have been dried and rolled. Pu-erh teas can be left to ferment for up to 20 years. As a result of this process, some pu-erh teas can retain their freshness for up to 50 years. Pu-erh became highly prized as a commodity for trading and is still sought after by officials, royalty, and tea connoisseurs.

Pu-erh teas undergo varying degrees of fermentation and can be classified as young raw pu-erh, aged raw pu-erh, or ripe pu-erh. Good-quality pu-erh tea has a deep, earthy flavor that goes well with decadent desserts and is often enjoyed primarily by coffee drinkers. Low-quality pu-erh can taste muddy.

Because of its purported health benefits for the digestive system, pu-erh is often had as a digestif after a rich or greasy meal, but it can be an acquired taste. If you're not particularly fond of it on its own, you can try a pu-erh blend that includes vanilla, ginger, and mint.

YOUNG RAW PU-ERH

Young raw pu-erh is fermented for less than three years and tastes similar to green tea. It can be sweet or bitter depending on the region where the tea plants are grown.

Young Raw Pu-erh Brew

Servings: 1

Steep Time: 5 minutes

Ingredients:

- 8 oz water plus a little more
- 1 tsp young raw pu-erh tea leaves

Directions:

1. Place the water in an electric kettle and boil to 212 °F.
2. Pour some of the water into the teapot and cup and swirl it around to warm up the teaware. Once they are warm, discard the water.
3. Add the pu-erh tea leaves to a tea strainer, then place it in your pot.
4. Pour the hot water over the leaves, then immediately remove the tea strainer.
5. Pour the tea into your pre-warmed cup and enjoy.
6. You can re-steep this tea many times.

AGED RAW PU-ERH AND RIPE PU-ERH

Aged raw pu-erh is fermented for a bit longer than young raw pu-erh and is darker in color with a hint of fruitiness. Ripe pu-erh is made by allowing the tea leaves to ferment in large piles (almost like composting) for months or years. This pu-erh is decadent and creamy with a touch of earthiness.

Ripe Pu-erh Tea

Servings: 1

Steep Time: 1–5 minutes

Ingredients:

- 8 oz water plus more
- 1 tsp ripe pu-erh tea leaves

Directions:

1. Place the water in an electric kettle and boil to 212 °F.
2. Pour some of the water into the teapot and cup and swirl it around to warm up the teaware. Once they are warm, discard the water.

3. Add your tea leaves to the teapot, then add some boiling water to rinse your pu-erh tea leaves. Swirl it around gently, then empty the water, ensuring the tea leaves remain.
4. Now pour the hot water over the leaves.
5. Allow the tea to steep for 5 minutes. The brewing time depends on your personal preference. You can experiment to find what works best for you.
6. Pour the tea into your pre-warmed cup and enjoy.
7. You can keep the leaves in the teapot and add more water, allowing it to brew longer. You should not let it steep for more than 2 hours.

PU-ERH, WESTERN STYLE

If you're relatively new to the world of tea, particularly pu-erh teas, this is a simple way to get started.

Western Pu-erh Brew

Servings: 1

Steep Time: 30 seconds to 4 minutes

Ingredients:

- 8 oz of water plus more
- 1 tsp pu-erh tea leaves

Directions:

1. Place the water in an electric kettle and boil to 212 °F.
2. Pour some of the water into the teapot and cup and swirl it around to warm up the teaware. Once they are warm, discard the water.
3. Add your tea leaves to a tea infuser, then place it in the teapot.
4. Add some boiling water over the leaves in the infuser to rinse your pu-erh tea leaves. Swirl it around gently, then empty the water, ensuring the tea leaves remain.
5. Now pour the hot water over the leaves and allow the tea to steep for 30 seconds to 4 minutes. The steeping time depends on your taste, so try tasting it at different intervals to figure out what works well.
6. Once steeped, remove the tea strainer and enjoy your cup of tea.
7. You can reuse the leaves for several more infusions.

Pu-erh is an incredibly unique tea experience. There is simply no other tea like it. It is complex yet smooth and full-bodied. Brewing the perfect cup of pu-erh tea depends on your personal taste. You can experiment with any of the methods shared to find the right fit for you. The most essential part of brewing a great pu-erh tea is ensuring you have fresh, high-quality leaves.

Once you've mastered the art of your perfect pu-erh brew, you can challenge yourself to find the right balance to have that delicate cup of white tea that is just right.

6

EXPERIENCE THE BLISS OF WHITE TEA

White tea originates from Fujian province in China. It is made from the tea plant's young leaves and new buds. It gets its name because of the white fuzz found on the young leaves that help to protect them from insects while they are growing.

White tea can be traced back about 1,500 years to the Tang dynasty (618–907). At that time, it was considered a special tea harvested only in the early spring so the pickers could get the silver needles. The young leaves were steamed, crushed, molded, and baked into cakes to dry. To brew the tea, you had to roast the cakes over a fire and crush it into a powder.

During the Song dynasty (960–1279), white tea became the tea of the royals. The tea was given in tribute to the emperor in powdered form. The powder was whisked in a bowl of hot water until it was frothy and then drunk (a process similar to making matcha). However, by the time of the Ming dynasty (1368–1644), it was decreed that only loose leaf white tea could be given in tribute to the emperor. This order forced the tea farmers to search for different methods of storing and preserving white tea, which is still used today.

White teas tend to be more expensive than other tea types because they are handpicked, and the harvesting time is much shorter than other types of tea. The young leaves for white tea are usually harvested between mid-March and early April. Once picked, the leaves are withered and dried immediately using natural light, heat vents, or drying chambers to prevent the leaves' oxidation.

There are five varieties of white tea: Bai Hao Yin Zhen, Bai Mu Dan, Shou Mei, Gong Mei, and Darjeeling white tea. The flavor profile of white teas can range from light and fruity to floral and sweet or even woodsy, depending on your variety of white tea. When brewed, the tea is normally pale yellow or gold with a floral aroma.

Many people believe that because white tea is so light, the caffeine level in a cup is lower than other teas, especially black teas. However, many variables can affect the degree of caffeine in your tea, including the variety of the tea plant (the *assamica* variety tends to have a higher caffeine content than the *sinensis* variety), the length of the growing season, the type of fertilizer used, and what part of the plant is harvested.

The tips of the tea leaves, particularly the young ones, tend to contain higher doses of caffeine. The plant uses this defense mechanism to protect its young leaves from being eaten by insects. The concentrated caffeine at the tips acts as a natural pesticide and kills any insects trying to take a bite out of the leaves. As such, white teas can potentially have higher levels of caffeine.

So don't discount a cup of white tea in the morning to boost your energy. Not to mention, white teas have a ton of antioxidants that can increase immune function, reduce stress, and support heart health. So why not give white tea a try?

BAI HAO YIN ZHEN

Also known as Silver Needle, Bai Hao Yin Zhen is the rarest and highest quality white tea. It is made from only the young buds of the tea plant. The shape of the buds must be the same, with no stems or leaves, and should have long, silvery tips like needles. The brewed tea is pale gold with a light, woody taste, and floral aroma.

Silver Needle Tea

Servings: 1

Steep Time: 3–5 minutes

Ingredients:

- 8 oz water
- 3–4 tsp Silver Needle tea leaves (add more leaves for a stronger tea)

Directions:

1. Place the water in an electric kettle and boil to 180 °F. If your water is too hot, you risk damaging your leaves, resulting in an astringent tea.
2. I recommend using a glass teapot to see the Silver Needle leaves floating in the water. Add the Silver Needle tea leaves to the teapot, then pour the hot water over the leaves. This is called "tea dancing" and is part of the experience of enjoying Silver Needle tea.
3. Allow the tea to steep for 3–5 minutes. The brewing time depends on your personal preference. You can experiment to find what works best for you.
4. Strain the brewed tea into your cup and enjoy.

BAI MU DAN

This white tea is also known as White Peony. It is another high-quality white tea made from the young buds of the tea plants, but each bud must have two young leaves attached to it. It is a deeper golden color with a nutty flavor. It is slightly bolder than the Silver Needle.

White Peony Tea

Servings: 1

Steep Time: 3–5 minutes

Ingredients:

- 8 oz water
- 2 tsp White Peony tea leaves

Directions:

1. Place the water in an electric kettle and boil to 180 °F. If your water is too hot, you risk damaging your leaves, resulting in a bitter tea. However, if the temperature is too low, your leaves will not steep properly, resulting in a watery flavor.
2. Add the White Peony tea leaves to the teapot, then pour the hot water over the leaves.
3. Allow the tea to steep for 3–5 minutes. The brewing time depends on your personal preference. You can experiment to find what works best for you.
4. Strain the brewed tea into your cup and enjoy.

SHOU MEI

Shou Mei or Long-Life Eyebrow is made from the leaves left on the tea plant after the highest-quality buds and leaves have been harvested for Silver Needle and White Peony teas. It is slightly more oxidized than the other white teas and has a darker color and flavor resembling an oolong tea.

As the story goes, two brothers lived in Nanking, China. They had inherited a tea garden from their father but were careless and too lazy to really work on the tea farm. They picked random buds and leaves of varying sizes, not paying attention to quality or consistency.

They were so lazy that they did not even want to process the leaves. As far as they were concerned, it was just too much work, so they dried the leaves in the sun immediately and let them cool in the shade. In this way, they accidentally discovered that by not processing the leaves, they preserved the white hairs on the leaves.

This new tea became incredibly popular, and the villagers were so fascinated that they tried to discover how the brothers made their tea. They tried spying on the brothers to learn their technique, but all they saw were the brothers drying the leaves in the sun. They didn't understand this was the secret—the brothers weren't processing the leaves.

Long-Life Eyebrow Tea

Servings: 1

Steep Time: 1–2 minutes

Ingredients:

- 8 oz water plus more
- 2 tsp Shou Mei tea leaves

Directions:

1. Place the water in an electric kettle and boil to 180 °F. If your water is too hot, you risk damaging your leaves, resulting in an astringent tea.
2. Pour some of the water into the teapot and cup and swirl it around to warm up the teaware. Once they are warm, discard the water.
3. I recommend using a glass teapot to see the leaves floating in the water. Add the Shou Mei tea leaves to the teapot, then pour the hot water over the leaves. This "tea dancing" is part of the experience of white tea.

4. Allow the tea to steep for 1–2 minutes. The brewing time depends on your personal preference. Experiment to find what works best for you.
5. Strain the brewed tea into your cup.
6. Before drinking your tea, take a moment to inhale the sweet fragrance of the tea, then take a sip.
7. You can infuse the leaves again but steep them slightly longer.

GONG MEI

Gong Mei, or Tribute Eyebrow, is made from only the young leaves of the tea plant. It is a darker tea with an intense fragrance and bold, thick flavor.

Tribute Eyebrow Tea

Servings: 1

Steep Time: 2–3 minutes

Ingredients:

- 8 oz water plus more
- 1 tsp Gong Mei tea leaves

Directions:

1. Place the water in an electric kettle and boil to 180 °F. If your water is too hot, you risk damaging your leaves, resulting in an astringent tea.
2. Pour some of the water into the teapot and cup and swirl it around to warm up the teaware. Once they are warm, discard the water.
3. Add the Gong Mei tea leaves to the teapot, then pour the hot water over the leaves.
4. Allow the tea to steep for 2–3 minutes. The brewing time depends on your personal preference. Experiment to find what works best for you.
5. Strain the brewed tea into your cup and enjoy.
6. This is a great tea to brew using the grandpa method.

DARJEELING WHITE TEA

Unlike the other white teas, this white tea comes from Darjeeling, India, as the name suggests. Although it is a white tea, it has a deeper color than other white teas. It is made from the fuzzy, young buds of the tea plant and has a sweet, creamy flavor profile with a hint of citrus.

White Darjeeling Brew

Servings: 1

Steep Time: 2–4 minutes

Ingredients:

- 8 oz water
- 2 tsp White Darjeeling tea leaves

Directions:

1. Place the water in an electric kettle and boil to 212 °F.
2. Add your leaves to a tea strainer and insert it into the teapot.
3. Pour some of the hot water over the leaves in the teapot.
4. Allow the tea to steep for 2–4 minutes. The brewing time depends on your personal preference. You can experiment to find what works best for you.
5. Pour the tea into your teacup and enjoy.
6. You can keep the leaves in the teapot and add more water for a second cup. You can infuse these leaves up to three times.

White tea may be the least processed of the teas, but they are certainly bursting with flavor. In general, white teas are light, sweet, and even delicate, but they can also be fruity and floral with even a hint of citrus. White teas are an experience for your senses. The aroma of the brewed tea soothes the soul, and that first sip relaxes the body and calms the mind. Visually, the "tea dancing" can be soothing and mesmerizing.

As we continue exploring this world of tea, we turn to herbal infusions. They may not be teas in the true sense, but they can bring that same level of comfort and relaxation.

7

PERFECTING HERBAL INFUSIONS

Many cultures worldwide believe herbal infusions have spiritual benefits and can be used to metaphorically open your mind to spiritual

connections. While herbal tea may seem like a new trend in most Western countries, herbal infusions can be traced back to the Shang dynasty in China about 4,000 years ago. Traditional Chinese medicine is well known for using herbal remedies to treat and cure innumerable illnesses and ailments. Herbal infusions as medicine are also commonplace in India, Egypt, and Greece.

Technically speaking, herbal tea cannot be considered a true tea since it does not come from the *Camellia sinensis* plant. It is, in fact, a tisane which is a blend of dried herbs, spices, flowers, or fruits added to water. In more and more instances, herbal infusions are being used as an alternative method for treating various illnesses, most probably because of the medicinal value of the dried ingredients found in herbal teas.

However, it is important to note that though herbal teas may have health benefits, some are simply flavored water with added sugar. Of course, some herbal teas legitimately have health-friendly components and have been used for centuries as medicine, but it is important to beware of the differences. Furthermore, herbal teas should be consumed in moderation and always with the approval of your medical practitioner since some herbal teas can be risky for those with certain health conditions. It is also important to note that herbal teas are not a substitute for proper medical care.

Herbal teas are great for relaxation and can form part of your self-care routine. Just be sure to check with your healthcare provider to ensure the herbal tea ingredients are safe for you.

Herbal teas come in countless varieties with unique flavors and aromas, but the major flavor profiles are sweet, aromatic, and bitter. Sweet herbal teas include those that have fruits or berries as well as some varieties of flowers. Aromatic teas have strong scents and flavors, including ginger, cinnamon, and turmeric. As the name suggests, bitter teas are astringent, like holy basil and fennel.

CHAMOMILE

Chamomile is an herb used for centuries as a natural treatment for various ailments. It has been used to treat nausea, heartburn, upset stomachs, indigestion, and vomiting. Chamomile tea is made from the dried flowers of the daisy-like Asteraceae plant family. In addition to inducing relaxation, chamomile can help to soothe your nervous system and allow for better sleep.

Warm Chamomile Tea

Servings: 2

Steep Time: 4–5 minutes

Ingredients:

- 2 cups water
- 3 tsp dried chamomile
- honey, optional

Directions:

1. Place the water in an electric kettle and boil to 212 °F.
2. Add the dried chamomile leaves to the teapot, then pour the hot water over the leaves and cover the pot.
3. Allow the tea to steep for 4–5 minutes.
4. Strain the brewed tea into your cup, add honey if using, and enjoy.
5. Try adding a splash of citrus, vanilla, or even some cinnamon to give your tea more flavor since chamomile is relatively mild.

Chamomile Latte

Servings: 2

Prep Time: 5 minutes

Cook Time: 15 minutes

Ingredients:

- 4 tsp dried chamomile
- 1 ½ cups water
- 1 tbsp honey
- 1 ½ cups milk of your choice
- ground cinnamon

Directions:

1. In a small saucepan, add the water and bring it to a boil over medium heat.
2. Once boiling, remove the pan and add the dried chamomile.
3. Cover the pot and allow the chamomile to brew for 10 minutes.
4. While the tea is brewing, add the milk to another saucepan and warm it over medium heat. Whisk the milk constantly until it is warm and frothy.

5. Once the tea is brewed, strain out the leaves and add honey to the brewed tea.
6. Divide the tea equally into two tea mugs, then add equal amounts of the warmed milk to each mug, reserving some of the foam.
7. Stir the liquids gently to combine.
8. Add the reserved foam to each mug, then dust with cinnamon before serving warm.

GINGER

This root is native to Asia and other tropical regions. Like chamomile, it has been used for thousands of years to treat illnesses, including coughs, colds, diabetes, nausea, and even arthritis. Ginger tea is probably one of the most common ways in which ginger is consumed. Compounds like gingerol found in ginger root can aid the body's immune response to inflammation. Ginger tea is often used to alleviate motion sickness and relieve menstrual cramps.

While ginger is generally considered safe to consume, you probably shouldn't be having it in large quantities. Too much ginger can cause bloating and heartburn, so it's best to enjoy it in moderation.

Ginger Tea

Servings: 2

Prep Time: 5 minutes

Cook Time: 20 minutes

Ingredients:

- 4 cups water
- 2 tbsp fresh ginger, peeled and thinly sliced
- 2 tbsp honey
- 1 tbsp fresh lime juice, optional

Directions:

1. In a saucepan, add the water and the ginger and bring them to a boil over medium heat. Let it boil for 10 minutes. For a more robust flavor, leave it for 20 minutes and use more slices of ginger.
2. Once the desired boiling time is complete, remove the pan from the water and strain the liquid into two tea mugs.
3. If using, add the honey and lime juice, and stir well to combine.
4. Enjoy your ginger tea warm.

Honey Ginger Latte

Servings: 1

Prep Time: 2 minutes

Cook Time: 4 minutes

Ingredients:

- 2 tbsp fresh ginger, grated
- 1 cinnamon stick
- 1 ½ cups milk of your choice
- 1 tsp honey
- ground cinnamon, for topping

Directions:

1. Add the ginger, cinnamon, and milk to a medium saucepan and place over medium heat.
2. Whisk the mixture continuously until it is warmed through and frothy. This should take about 3–4 minutes.
3. Once the milk is warm, remove the pan from the heat and add the honey. Stir until the honey has dissolved completely.
4. Strain the ginger latte into a mug and sprinkle with ground cinnamon.

HIBISCUS

This edible flowering plant is native to tropical regions, including Africa, Asia, Central America, and the Caribbean. When brewed, the tea is tart, similar to cranberries. The flowers of the hibiscus plant are usually brightly colored, but did you know that it's not the petals that are eaten? It's the sepals that are dried and used in cooking.

Hibiscus is becoming increasingly popular as a tea because of its high antioxidant properties. This high level of antioxidants gives the tea its rich red color. The antioxidants help to prevent and protect your cells from damage and disease. It can also aid in reducing blood pressure and the fat in your blood.

Additionally, hibiscus tea seems to have some antiviral properties that can protect against some strains of the avian flu. It can also help those suffering from high cholesterol because the components in the hibiscus tea can reduce LDL (bad) cholesterol levels.

Hibiscus Tea

Servings: 1

Steep Time: 4–5 minutes

Ingredients:

- 3 tsp dried hibiscus flowers
- 8 oz water
- honey or agave to taste, optional

Directions:

1. Boil the water in a kettle.
2. Place the dried hibiscus petals in a teapot, then pour the hot water over them.
3. Cover the teapot and allow the petals to brew for 4–5 minutes.
4. Strain the tea into a cup and add honey or agave, if using, and stir gently to combine.
5. Take a moment to inhale the fragrance before taking your first sip.

Iced Hibiscus Tea

Servings: 4

Prep Time: 10 minutes

Cook Time: 25 minutes

Ingredients:

- 4 cups water
- ½ cinnamon stick
- 2 pieces of ginger, thinly sliced
- ½ cup sugar
- ½ cup dried hibiscus petals
- lime slices, optional

Directions:

1. In a saucepan, add 2 cups of the water with the cinnamon, ginger, and sugar. Heat the mixture until the sugar is completely dissolved and it comes to a boil.
2. Remove the pan from the heat and add the dried hibiscus petal. Stir gently, then cover and let it steep for about 20 minutes.
3. Strain the steeped tea into a pitcher and discard the leaves and spices left in the strainer.

4. Add the remaining 2 cups of water to the hibiscus concentrate and mix well.
5. Place the pitcher of hibiscus tea in the refrigerator to chill for a few hours.
6. Serve over ice and garnish with a lime slice.

MINT

Mint was brought to the United States by the colonists and used as a treatment for gas, indigestion, upset stomachs, and headaches. It is also excellent for stomach pains and menstrual discomfort. The properties in the mint leaves relax the muscles of the digestive tract providing a kind of anesthetic effect on the walls of the stomach. As a result of this relaxation, any stomach pain and digestive issues are relieved. Mint tea alone does not have any caffeine, but it can provide a natural boost to your body and reduce tiredness while increasing mental acuity.

Mint tea is sweet but spicy at the same time. It has a very smooth texture, and it is not bitter.

Mint Tea

Servings: 2

Prep Time: 5 minutes

Cook Time: 5 minutes

Ingredients:

- 2 cups water
- 1 cup fresh mint leaves
- 2 tsp honey, optional
- 2 slices lemon, optional

Directions:

1. Place water in a saucepan and bring to a boil over medium heat.
2. When the water begins to boil, remove the pan from the heat and add the fresh mint leaves.
3. Allow the leaves to steep for about 3–5 minutes. The longer the leaves steep, the stronger the tea will be.
4. Strain the mint tea into two cups, add the honey if using, and stir well to combine.
5. Add a slice of lemon to the tea and serve warm.

ROOIBOS

Also known as red bush tea, rooibos has been grown and used in South Africa for centuries. Rooibos tea is made from the leaves of the shrub *Aspalathus linearis*. As such, it is an herb and not a tea in the true sense. Rooibos leaves are traditionally fermented after harvesting, which gives them their reddish-brown color. Green rooibos tea is not fermented but is usually more expensive than traditional rooibos.

Traditional rooibos is taken just like black tea, but green rooibos has more of a grassy flavor profile, making it similar to traditional green tea. It is a robust tea that is a great caffeine-free alternative to black and green teas and is loaded with antioxidants.

Rooibos Tea

Servings: 1

Steep Time: 10 minutes

Ingredients:

- 8 oz water
- 1 tsp rooibos tea leaves
- 1 tsp brown sugar
- milk, optional

Directions:

1. Place the water in an electric kettle and boil to 200 °F.
2. Add the rooibos tea leaves to the teapot, then pour the hot water over the leaves.
3. Cover the teapot and allow the tea to steep for 10 minutes.
4. Once steeped, strain the leaves and pour the tea into your teacup.
5. Add the sugar and milk, if using, and stir well.
6. Enjoy it warm.

Rooibos Iced Latte

Servings: 1

Prep Time: 3 minutes

Cook Time: 2 minutes

Ingredients:

- 2 tsp rooibos tea leaves
- ¾ cup water
- 1 tsp honey
- ½ tsp vanilla
- ¾ cup milk of your choice
- ice

Directions:

1. In a saucepan, add the water and bring it to a boil over medium heat.
2. Once the water is boiling, remove the pan from the heat and add the rooibos tea leaves.
3. Allow the tea to brew for about 3 minutes.
4. Strain the brewed tea into a glass, then add the honey and vanilla to the tea and mix well until the honey has dissolved completely.
5. Add the ice to the tea, then pour the milk over the ice.
6. Stir everything well and serve chilled.

ECHINACEA

This herb, also called purple coneflower, is one of the most popular herbs globally but is native to North America. Three of the nine species are used as herbal remedies, and it is most commonly used for treating colds and flu but has been used by Native Americans for centuries as a remedy for many illnesses.

Like other herbal teas, echinacea is loaded with antioxidants that help boost the body's immune response to fight off colds and flu effectively. It also contains specific compounds that work to reduce feelings of stress and anxiety.

You can enjoy echinacea on its own or blend it with black tea leaves for a refreshing drink. On its own, echinacea can be strong with a very earthy taste and a hint of floral. The medicinal compounds in the echinacea can produce a tingling effect on your tongue. Combining it with other herbs or tea leaves can make it a bit more palatable.

Echinacea Tea

Servings: 1

Steep Time: 15 minutes

Ingredients:

- 8 oz water
- 1 tsp dried echinacea tea
- honey, optional

Directions:

1. Place the water in an electric kettle and boil to 200 °F.
2. Add the echinacea tea leaves to the teapot, then pour the hot water over the leaves.
3. Cover the teapot and allow the tea to steep for 15 minutes.

4. Once steeped, strain the leaves and pour the tea into your teacup.
5. Add the honey, if using, and stir well until the honey has dissolved.
6. Enjoy it warm.

A warm cup of herbal tea can lift your spirit and soothe your senses. It can help when you're feeling overwhelmed and give you the boost you need to get on with your day. Many other herbal teas are available, but these are just some of the more popular and tested ones. Of course, it is always wise to check with your doctor to ensure that the herbal tea ingredients are safe for you to use in your particular circumstance.

Now that you've mastered all the true teas and the herbal teas, it's time to have some fun! In the next chapter, we will try our skills at making our tea blends. Being a tea purist is awesome, but sometimes it's nice to mix things up a little, so let's get on with it.

8

DIY TEA BLENDS

Tea can help us through tough times. We drink it when we celebrate; we embrace it when we're sad. It is the most versatile of drinks. Tea simply makes life a little better. So making your own tea would be tons of fun. You get to experiment with your favorite teas and herbs, and you work with your hands to create something new and uniquely you.

Many tea blends are done with herbs and spices but can include traditional black, green, and white teas to boost the blend. A range of teas on the market help with various ailments and concerns, but making your own blend gives you the freedom to care for your body in the way that feels and works best for you. Nobody knows what you need better than you do.

Before we begin making those blends, we'll learn a few of the basics about blending herbs. After all, creating tea is an art. Every herb you use is unique with its flavor profile, aroma, texture, and character.

WHAT IS A TEA BLEND?

Generally, a tea blend is a medley of teas and other ingredients like herbs and spices to create a new flavor. Tea blends can be very simple but unique to the creator. Some blends have only natural, raw ingredients, while others include essential oils and flavorings. For instance, Earl Grey tea, as you know, is a blend of black tea (traditionally Assam or Ceylon) and the essential oils from bergamot oranges. Sometimes flavors are added to the dried herb or fruit to bring out the taste of the herb.

A tea blend usually has a true tea base, but often dried herbs and fruits can be used as the base without actually using any true teas. Most true tea blends have a green or black tea base, but you can sometimes find blends with other true teas as their bases. It will be caffeinated if you're using true teas in your blend. Dried fruits and herbs or rooibos only will create a caffeine-free blend since they do not come from the tea plant.

Blending tea is about personal preferences and personal tastes, but a truly excellent tea blend will have a good balance. This means that when you blend your tea, you should aim to create harmony between your base, middle, and top flavor profiles. A seamless union of the ingredients creates a very satisfying experience for the tea drinker. Having said this, it will take quite a bit of practice and experimentation to reach that level, but that's the fun part!

FINDING YOUR HERBS AND TEAS

One of the key steps to a good-quality blend is where you get your herbs. If you have your own garden, then that's the best. If not, try to source your herbs locally to ensure freshness and maximum nutrient value. In the tea industry, like the wine industry, the term *terroir* is used to describe how the conditions in the growing region impact the tea or herb. Depending on the soil, weather, and general climate, the same herb grown in different places will vary slightly in flavor, color, and strength.

Choosing an herb grown locally means that the herb is specifically adapted to your region and experiences the same weather and climate conditions that you do. An herb grown closer to home will be infinitely better for you than one from farther away. Not to mention, supporting your small-scale farmers is always the way to go. Buying local means that you are contributing to the local biodiversity and ensuring future jobs in agriculture. Sometimes the local market can be inconsistent, and you do have to rely on imported products but do your research. Find sellers who adhere to fair trade standards and ethical practices.

In terms of teas, try to find a local small business that sources its tea leaves from fair trade and organic-certified companies and tea farms. With small businesses, you have a better chance of knowing where your tea is coming from and how it has been grown. Chances are you may even be able to get single-source tea leaves. It may take some work, but it will be worth it when you blend your first cup of tea.

EQUIPMENT NEEDED

If you're making small batches, you probably have most of the stuff you'll need at home. The most important thing you'll need is a digital scale. This is important for consistency in measuring dried herbs and tea leaves. Teaspoon measures are not quite as accurate. You will also need mixing bowls of different sizes and a spoon (wooden or stainless steel). It's great to have a notebook on hand when you're experimenting to write down your blends and keep track of what you've done.

Lastly, consider investing in some small opaque airtight containers or mason jars. You can use resealable opaque plastic bags, but they do not work quite as well. Whichever you choose, make sure that they seal well. Teas and herbs tend to absorb the smells around them, so if you store your blends near something with a strong aroma and the seal is not airtight, it will alter your blend's taste.

SETTING UP YOUR WORKSPACE

It goes with saying that the best place to set up is a table or counter that is clean and mess-free. Bear in mind you will generate a bit of herb dust when blending, so a space without clutter will be easier to clean. You can always work outdoors if you're in a warmer climate or during the warmer months. It will have great ventilation, and being outdoors adds another soothing element to making your own blends.

When you find your workspace, make sure it's somewhere you feel comfortable and can relax while creating your blends. Set up all your equipment close to you so you don't have to hunt for anything.

READY TO BLEND

Like anything else you do in the kitchen before you begin, ensure that your hands and equipment are clean and dry. When working with fresh herbs, any moisture can cause your herbs to spoil.

When adding your herbs or tea leaves to your blend, weighing them one at a time in the small mixing bowl is best to transfer them to the larger bowl. Depending on your batch size, try to find a bowl that can fix everything.

You can blend herbs and tea with your hands or a wooden or stainless steel spoon. Mix everything slowly, going in a circular motion to ensure it blends evenly. If you mix too fast, you will end up with herb dust everywhere which is a pain to clean up after. The smaller the batch, the less chance you will have too much of a mess.

BLENDING YOUR TEA

Because this is unique to you, you need to pay attention to what you need and your preferences regarding taste, texture, and experience. You're making a tea for you, so be confident and trust, but in case you need some help, here are a few tips:

1. Simple blend or complex one?

As a beginner, you may want to start with a simple blend and work your way up to more complex ones as you become more comfortable with the flavors and aromas. As the name suggests, a simple blend is two or three ingredients and can even be just a blend of pure teas. A complex one will include three or more ingredient and additional flavors.

2. Know the taste.

For each ingredient, you plan on using in your blend, steep it and taste it separately. This could be anything from pure tea to lavender to ginger. This step is critical as it will help you understand the flavor profiles of the individual components and decide whether they will work well together. Also, remember that blending two different types of pure tea may require different brewing temperatures, so you have to find a middle ground that can work well for both. With dried herbs, ensure that they are safe for you to use.

3. Weighing is important.

For every 8-oz cup of tea, you will need about 1 tsp (2 ½–3 g) of your tea blend. So it is important to weigh each ingredient individually before adding it to your mixing bowl. All the ingredients combined should equal 1 tsp. Try making a few variations of the same blend by slightly altering the amounts of the ingredients. You may not believe it, but a tiny ingredient adjustment can make a huge difference in flavor. Be sure to track how much of each component you add to each bowl. This way, you can try a few variations of the same blend and decide which one you like best.

4. Think about the end product.

When blending your tea, consider how you would like the final result to be had and how best you can highlight the components of the tea. Do you want to have the blend with milk? Is it for a specific purpose like energy or wellness? Would a particular sweetener bring out specific flavors? All these questions are important to ensure everything comes together cohesively and give you an excellent result. This should be fun, too, so go ahead and experiment a bit.

5. Take tons of notes.

We've already listed a notebook as part of the needed equipment, so remember to have it with you when you're blending your tea. You need to keep track of all the measurements and ingredients of your various blends, but just as importantly, you should note the taste, texture, aroma, look, and feel of the tea and the leaves of every blend you make. Was it too strong or too weak? Was it oily or astringent? All of these can help you to perfect your tea-blending skills. So make sure always to have that notebook and pen close by.

Depending on your blend, you'll have to choose ingredients that match that flavor profile. Add cardamom, cayenne, ginger, or cinnamon to your mix for a spicy blend. Add dried berries, apples, pears, or even citrus peel if you want something fruity. Choose sage, chamomile, or echinacea if you're craving that grassy, herby taste. For a floral brew, go for lavender, rose, or rosemary.

If you're buying fresh herbs and fruits, you will have to dehydrate them to remove all the water content. You can do this by using a dehydrator or naturally drying the herbs and plants by hanging them upside down in a dark, dry place for up to a few weeks. Remember to store your dried herbs and fruits in airtight containers away from light.

TEA BLEND RECIPES

Now that you have all the basics, you're eager to start. You can jump right into experimenting with your own blends, but if you're a little unsure or want to try out some blends before doing your own, then keep reading.

I've put together some blends to help you get started. Some are simple, and some are a bit more complex. Of course, feel free to adjust the measurements in these recipes to suit your own tastes or to learn what differences small adjustments in ingredients can make to the flavor of your tea.

BLACK TEA BLENDS

Rosy Morning Blend

Servings: 6 servings

Prep Time: 5 minutes

Ingredients:

- 3 tsp Assam tea leaves
- 2 tsp Darjeeling tea leaves
- 1 tsp rosebuds, dried

Directions:

1. Add all the ingredients to a mixing bowl and mix carefully until everything is well blended.
2. To use, brew 1 tsp of the tea blend in 8 oz of hot water and allow it to steep for 3–4 minutes, then strain and enjoy.
3. Store the tea blend in an airtight container for up to one year.

Lavender Earl Grey

Servings: 5 servings

Prep Time: 5 minutes

Ingredients:

- 4 tsp Earl Grey tea leaves
- 1 tsp lavender, dried

Directions:

1. Add all the ingredients to a mixing bowl and mix carefully until everything is well blended.
2. To use, brew 1 tsp of the tea blend in 8 oz of hot water and allow it to steep for 3–4 minutes, then strain and enjoy.
3. Store the tea blend in an airtight container for up to one year.

Warm Spice Blend

Servings: 24

Prep Time: 5 minutes

Ingredients:

- ½ cup black tea leaves of your choice
- 1 tsp cinnamon
- ½ tsp ground clove
- 1 tsp ground ginger
- ½ tsp ground cardamom
- ¼ cup rose petals, dried

Directions:

1. Add all the ingredients to a mixing bowl and mix carefully until everything is well blended.
2. To use, brew 1 tsp of the tea blend in 8 oz of hot water and allow it to steep for 3–4 minutes, then strain and enjoy.
3. Store the tea blend in an airtight container for up to one year.

Orange Tea

Servings: 48

Prep Time: 5 minutes

Ingredients:

- 1 ½ cups Assam tea leaves
- 1 tbsp ground cinnamon
- ½ cup orange peel, dried and chopped

Directions:

1. Add all the ingredients to a mixing bowl and mix carefully until everything is well blended.
2. To use, brew 1 tsp of the tea blend in 8 oz of hot water and allow it to steep for 5 minutes, then strain and enjoy.
3. Store the tea blend in an airtight container for up to one month.

GREEN TEA BLENDS

Minty Green

Servings: 4

Prep Time: 5 minutes

Ingredients:

- 2 tsp sencha green tea
- 1 tsp lemongrass, dried
- 1 tsp mint, dried

Directions:

1. Add all the ingredients to a mixing bowl and mix carefully until everything is well blended.
2. To use, brew 1 tsp of the tea blend in 8 oz of hot water and allow it to steep for 2 minutes, then strain and enjoy.
3. Store the tea blend in an airtight container for up to one month.

Green Ginger

Servings: 4 servings

Prep Time: 5 minutes

Ingredients:

- 4 tsp green tea leaves
- 1 tsp ginger, dried

Directions:

1. Add all the ingredients to a mixing bowl and mix carefully until everything is well blended.
2. To use, brew 1 tsp of the tea blend in 8 oz of hot water and allow it to steep for 2 minutes, then strain and enjoy.
3. Store the tea blend in an airtight container for up to one month.

Raspberry Green Tea

Servings: 20

Prep Time: 5 minutes

Ingredients:

- 18 tsp green tea leaves
- 1 tsp raspberries, dried
- 1 tsp hibiscus flowers, dried

Directions:

1. Add all the ingredients to a mixing bowl and mix carefully until everything is well blended.
2. To use, brew 1 tsp of the tea blend in 8 oz of hot water and allow it to steep for 5 minutes, then strain and enjoy.
3. Store the tea blend in an airtight container for up to one month.

Lemon Green Tea

Servings: 20

Prep Time: 5 minutes

Ingredients:

- ½ cup green tea leaves
- ½ cup lemon balm, dried and crushed
- 2 tbsp fennel
- 1 tsp ground ginger

Directions:

1. Add all the ingredients to a mixing bowl and mix carefully until everything is well blended.
2. To use, brew 1 tsp of the tea blend in 8 oz of hot water and allow it to steep for 5 minutes, then strain and enjoy.
3. Store the tea blend in an airtight container for up to one month.

OOLONG TEA BLENDS

Spring Delight

Servings: 32

Prep Time: 5 minutes

Ingredients:

- 8 tbsp oolong tea leaves
- 8 tbsp nettle leaf, dried
- 8 tbsp fennel, dried
- 4 tbsp rose petals, dried
- 4 tbsp mint, dried

Directions:

1. Add all the ingredients to a mixing bowl and mix carefully until everything is well blended.
2. To use, brew 1 tsp of the tea blend in 12 oz of hot water and allow it to steep for 3 minutes, then strain and enjoy.
3. Store the tea blend in an airtight container for up to one month.

Peach Oolong

Servings: 3 servings

Prep Time: 5 minutes

Ingredients:

- 6 tsp oolong tea leaves
- 3 tsp candied peach, chopped

Directions:

1. Add all the ingredients to a mixing bowl and mix carefully until everything is well blended.
2. To use, brew 1 ½ tsp of the tea blend in 8 oz of hot water and allow it to steep for 3 minutes, then strain and enjoy.
3. Store the tea blend in an airtight container for up to one month.

Coconut Surprise

Servings: 4

Prep Time: 5 minutes

Ingredients:

- 9 tsp oolong tea leaves
- 4 ½ tsp coconut, dried and shredded

Directions:

1. Add all the ingredients to a mixing bowl and mix carefully until everything is well blended.
2. To use, brew 1 ½ tsp of the tea blend in 8 oz of hot water and allow it to steep for 3 minutes, then strain and enjoy.
3. Store the tea blend in an airtight container for up to one month.

Cinnamon Apple Oolong

Servings: 8

Prep Time: 5 minutes

Ingredients:

- 8 tsp oolong tea leaves
- 4 tsp dried apple, chopped
- 2 tsp cinnamon bark pieces

Directions:

1. Add all the ingredients to a mixing bowl and mix carefully until everything is well blended.
2. To use, brew 1 ½ tsp of the tea blend in 8 oz of hot water and allow it to steep for 3 minutes, then strain and enjoy.
3. Store the tea blend in an airtight container for up to one month.

WHITE TEA BLENDS

Fruity White

Servings: 20

Prep Time: 5 minutes

Ingredients:

- 11 tbsp white tea leaves
- ½ cup strawberries, dried
- ½ cup apples, dried
- ½ cup orange peel, dried
- ½ cup rose petals, dried

Directions:

1. Add all the ingredients to a mixing bowl and mix carefully until everything is well blended.
2. To use, brew 2 tbsp of the tea blend in 8 oz of hot water and allow it to steep for 10 minutes, then strain and enjoy.
3. Store the tea blend in an airtight container for up to one month.

Spicy White

Servings: 2

Prep Time: 5 minutes

Ingredients:

- 4 tsp white tea leaves
- 2 tsp strawberries, dried
- 1 tsp peppercorns

Directions:

1. Add all the ingredients to a mixing bowl and mix carefully until everything is well blended.
2. To use, brew 2 tsp of the tea blend in 8 oz of hot water and allow it to steep for 10 minutes, then strain and enjoy.
3. Store the tea blend in an airtight container for up to one month.

White Berry Blend

Servings: 2

Prep Time: 5 minutes

Ingredients:

- 2 tsp cedar berries
- 2 tbsp white peony tea leaves

Directions:

1. Add all the ingredients to a mixing bowl and mix carefully until everything is well blended.
2. To use, brew 1 tbsp of the tea blend in 8 oz of hot water and allow it to steep for 10 minutes, then strain and enjoy.
3. Store the tea blend in an airtight container for up to one month.

Valentine White

Servings: 2

Prep Time: 5 minutes

Ingredients:

- 2 tbsp white tea leaves
- 2 tsp rose petals, dried

Directions:

1. Add all the ingredients to a mixing bowl and mix carefully until everything is well blended.
2. To use, brew 1 tbsp of the tea blend in 8 oz of hot water and allow it to steep for 10 minutes, then strain and enjoy.
3. Store the tea blend in an airtight container for up to one month.

PU-ERH BLENDS

Island Pu-erh

Servings: 10

Prep Time: 10 minutes

Ingredients:

- 4 tsp ripe pu-erh tea leaves
- 2 tsp coconut, shredded
- 2 tsp candied pineapple, chopped
- 2 tsp candied mango, chopped

Directions:

1. Add all the ingredients to a mixing bowl and mix carefully until everything is well blended.
2. To use, brew 1 tsp of the tea blend in 8 oz of hot water and allow it to steep for 5 minutes, then strain and enjoy.
3. Store the tea blend in an airtight container for up to one month.

Citrus Pu-erh

Servings: 12

Prep Time: 5 minutes

Ingredients:

- 8 tsp ripe pu-erh tea leaves
- 4 tsp orange peel, dried and chopped

Directions:

1. Add all the ingredients to a mixing bowl and mix carefully until everything is well blended.
2. To use, brew 1 tsp of the tea blend in 8 oz of hot water and allow it to steep for 5 minutes, then strain and enjoy.
3. Store the tea blend in an airtight container for up to one month.

Jasmine Pu-erh

Servings: 10

Prep Time: 5 minutes

Ingredients:

- 8 tsp ripe pu-erh tea leaves
- 2 tsp jasmine, dried and crumbled

Directions:

1. Add all the ingredients to a mixing bowl and mix carefully until everything is well blended.
2. To use, brew 1 tsp of the tea blend in 8 oz of hot water and allow it to steep for 5 minutes, then strain and enjoy.
3. Store the tea blend in an airtight container for up to one month.

Earthy Pu-erh

Servings: 8

Prep Time: 5 minutes

Ingredients:

- 6 tsp black tea leaves of your choice
- 2 tsp pu-erh tea leaves

Directions:

1. Add all the ingredients to a mixing bowl and mix carefully until everything is well blended.
2. To use, brew 1 tsp of the tea blend in 8 oz of hot water and allow it to steep for 3 minutes, then strain and enjoy.
3. Store the tea blend in an airtight container for up to one month.

HERBAL BLENDS

Sleepy Time Tea

Servings: 84

Prep Time: 5 minutes

Ingredients:

- ¼ cup rose petals, dried
- ½ cup lemon balm, dried
- 1 tbsp lavender, dried
- 1 cup chamomile, dried

Directions:

1. Add all the ingredients to a mixing bowl and mix carefully until everything is well blended.
2. To use, brew 1 tsp of the tea blend in 8 oz of hot water and allow it to steep for 5–15 minutes, then strain and enjoy.
3. Store the tea blend in an airtight container for up to one year.

Winter Warmth

Servings: 8

Prep Time: 10 minutes

Ingredients:

- ¼ cup cocoa powder
- ½ cup peppermint tea leaves
- 2 tbsp cacao nibs, finely chopped

Directions:

1. Sift the cocoa powder into a bowl then add the other ingredients and mix carefully until everything is well blended.
2. To use, brew 1 tsp of the tea blend in 8 oz of hot water and allow it to steep for 5–10 minutes, then strain and enjoy.
3. Store the tea blend in an airtight container until ready to use.

Immune-Boosting Blend

Servings: 4

Prep Time: 5 minutes

Ingredients:

- 1 cup echinacea, dried
- 4 tsp mint leaves, dried
- 4 tsp lemongrass, dried

Directions:

1. Add all the ingredients to a mixing bowl and mix carefully until everything is well blended.
2. To use, brew ¼ cup of the tea blend in 8 oz of hot water and allow it to steep for 15 minutes, then strain and enjoy.
3. Store the tea blend in an airtight container for up to one year.

Summertime Blend

Servings: 4

Prep Time: 5 minutes

Ingredients:

- 4 tsp hibiscus, dried
- 2 tsp lemongrass, dried
- 2 tsp mint leaves, dried

Directions:

1. Add all the ingredients to a mixing bowl and mix carefully until everything is well blended.
2. To use, brew 1 tsp of the tea blend in 8 oz of hot water and allow it to steep for 5–15 minutes, then strain and enjoy.
3. Store the tea blend in an airtight container for up to one year.

ROOIBOS BLENDS

Citrus Rooibos

Servings: 4

Prep Time: 5 minutes

Ingredients:

- 4 tbsp red rooibos
- 4 tsp orange peel, dried
- 4 tsp lemon peel, dried

Directions:

1. Add all the ingredients to a mixing bowl and mix carefully until everything is well blended.
2. To use, brew 1 tsp of the tea blend in 12 oz of hot water and allow it to steep for 5–10 minutes, then strain and enjoy.
3. Store the tea blend in an airtight container for up to one year.

Chamomile Rooibos

Servings: 4

Prep Time: 5 minutes

Ingredients:

- 4 tbsp red rooibos
- 4 tsp chamomile flowers, dried
- 2 tsp rose hips, dried
- 2 tsp rose petals, dried

Directions:

1. Add all the ingredients to a mixing bowl and mix carefully until everything is well blended.
2. To use, brew 1 tbsp of the tea blend in 12 oz of hot water and allow it to steep for 5–10 minutes, then strain and enjoy.
3. Store the tea blend in an airtight container for up to one year.

Rooibos Dreams

Servings: 4

Prep Time: 5 minutes

Ingredients:

- 4 tbsp green rooibos
- 4 tsp peppermint, dried
- 4 tsp lemon verbena, dried

Directions:

1. Add all the ingredients to a mixing bowl and mix carefully until everything is well blended.
2. To use, brew 1 tbsp of the tea blend in 12 oz of hot water and allow it to steep for 5–10 minutes, then strain and enjoy.
3. Store the tea blend in an airtight container for up to one year.

Vanilla Rooibos

Servings: 24 servings

Prep Time: 10 minutes

Ingredients:

- 6 ½ tbsp rooibos tea
- 5 tsp dried fruit (apples, dates, raisins)
- 1 vanilla bean

Directions:

1. Add the rooibos to a medium-sized bowl, then slice the vanilla bean and scrape the seeds into the bowl with the rooibos.
2. Cut the vanilla pod into small pieces using kitchen scissors and add it to the bowl.
3. Now cut the dried fruit into small pieces and place them in the bowl.
4. Carefully blend all the ingredients and store them in an airtight container. Let the blend rest for a few days before using it for best results.
5. To brew, add 1 tsp of the tea blend to 8 oz of hot water and steep for 10 minutes. Strain and enjoy warm.

Blending your own teas is a great way to take some time from your busy life to slow down and enjoy the aromas, textures, and experience of creating something new just for you. It's an excellent way to embrace self-care and well-being. Whether you use one of the recipes here or make your own, each tea you create is unique to you and your story. If you pay close attention, it may even be exactly what you need at that given moment. It's also a stress-free way to create it together with family and friends. So give it a try. You might be surprised that it is equal parts fun and relaxing. Even more fun is the tea cocktails we get to try in our next chapter.

9

TEA COCKTAILS

Did you know that some of the earliest versions of iced tea in the United States were green teas generously spiked with alcohol? In the southern states, they were called tea punches, and the tea was brewed hot and left to cool before adding the alcohol. If you could afford ice, it was added to the cooled tea. In the 19th century, Regent's Punch, named for King George VI, called for champagne to be added to the brewed tea.

Tea-infused cocktails make light, delicious, and refreshing drinks that produce the right amount of punch. From all that we've discussed so far, you know that each tea is distinct, and adding it to your cocktails can provide a nice boost while also completing your choice of alcohol.

Not to mention, they're so fun to make.

We've kept the recipes in this section low in sugar and used natural ingredients as much as possible. We've opted for dried versions of the spice or fruit for many of the recipes, but you can use fresh alternatives. Just note that fresh ingredients will have a more robust flavor, so you may need to adjust the amounts used in the recipe accordingly. Also, tea brewed for cocktails needs to be stronger than you would normally make it. This ensures that the flavor of the tea is preserved when the other cocktail ingredients are added.

Unlike other cocktails, tea cocktails shouldn't be shaken with ice because it will dilute the cocktail quickly. For most of the cocktail recipes, we will be cold brewing the tea since there's less chance of over-steeping the tea. Not to mention, a cold brew would mean you get your cold cocktail quicker.

The recipes in this section are just for inspiration and to show you that tea can be something other than serious business. Have a party and experiment with the flavors and quantities. You can also omit the alcohol to create kid-friendly mocktails. There is no right or wrong way here. Just have fun and find what suits your mood.

TEA-BASED COCKTAILS

White Tea Mule With Lemongrass

Servings: 1

Prep Time: 15 minutes

Ingredients:

Tea Base

- 5 oz water, room temperature
- ½ tsp dried peach
- ½ tsp lemongrass, chopped
- 1 tsp white tea leaves

Cocktail

- ¾ tbsp agave
- 1 ½ oz vodka
- 3 ½ oz tea base
- 3 oz ginger beer
- ice
- 1 slice ginger

Directions:

1. To make the tea base, add the dried peach, lemongrass, and white tea leaves to a tea ball, then place it in the water. Allow the tea to brew for 10 minutes, moving the tea ball from time to time. Once brewed, remove the tea ball from the water.
2. In a shaker, add 3 ½ oz of the tea base, the agave, and the vodka. Shake until the agave is fully dissolved.
3. Add the ice to a glass, pour the tea mixture over the ice, and stir gently to chill the mixture.
4. Add the ginger beer and stir again.
5. Garnish with the ginger slice and serve chilled.

Lavender Peppermint Twist

Servings: 1

Prep Time: 15 minutes

Ingredients:

Tea Base

- 6 oz water, room temperature
- 1 tsp dried peppermint
- 1 tsp lemongrass, chopped

Cocktail

- ½ oz lavender simple syrup
- 1 ½ oz vodka
- 4 oz tea base
- a dash of lemon juice
- ice

Directions:

1. Place the water in a cup.
2. Add the peppermint and lemongrass to a tea ball and place it in the cup of water. Allow the tea to brew for 10 minutes, then remove the tea ball.

3. In a shaker, add 4 oz of the tea base, the lavender syrup, the vodka, and the lemon juice. Shake to combine all the ingredients.
4. Add the ice to the shaker and stir gently to chill the cocktail.
5. Pour the cocktail into a glass and enjoy chilled.

Spike Grey

Servings: 1

Prep Time: 15 minutes

Ingredients:

Tea Base

- 6 oz water, room temperature
- ½ tsp dried lavender
- 1 ½ tsp Earl Grey tea leaves

Cocktail

- ½ oz elderflower liqueur (you can substitute this with rose water)
- 1 ½ oz vodka
- 4 oz tea base
- 1 lemon slice

Directions:

1. To make the tea base, add the dried lavender and Earl Grey tea leaves to a tea ball, then place it in room-temperature water.
2. Allow the tea to brew for 10 minutes, stirring the tea ball from time to time. Once brewed, remove the tea ball from the water.
3. In a shaker, add 4 oz of the tea base, the elderflower liqueur, and the vodka. Shake gently to combine.
4. Add the ice to a glass, then strain the tea mixture over the ice. Swirl the glass gently to chill the mixture.
5. Garnish with the lemon slice and serve chilled.

Berry Simple

Servings: 1

Prep Time: 15 minutes

Ingredients:

Tea Base

- 6 oz water, room temperature
- ¼ tsp rose petals

- 1 tsp mix of dried raspberries, dried blueberries, and dried strawberries
- 1 tsp rooibos

Cocktail

- ½ tbsp agave
- ½ oz rose simple syrup
- 1 ½ oz vodka
- 4 ½ oz tea base
- ice
- fresh raspberries

Directions:

1. To make the tea base, add the dried berry mix, rose petals, and rooibos tea leaves to a tea ball, then place it in room temperature water. Allow the tea to brew for 10 minutes, moving the tea ball from time to time. Once brewed, remove the tea ball from the water.
2. In a shaker, add 4 ½ oz of the tea base, the agave, the rose syrup, and the vodka. Shake until the agave dissolves completely.
3. Add the ice to the shaker and swirl gently to chill the mixture, then pour into a glass.

4. Garnish with the fresh raspberries and serve chilled.

Tropical Delight

Servings: 1

Prep Time: 15 minutes

Ingredients:

Tea Base

- 6 oz water, room temperature
- ½ tsp unsweetened coconut, shredded
- ½ tsp dried orange peel
- 1 tsp lemongrass, chopped

Cocktail

- 1 oz pineapple juice
- 1 tbsp agave
- 1 ½ oz vodka
- 3 ½ oz tea base
- ice
- 1 pineapple wedge

Directions:

1. To make the tea base, add the shredded coconut, orange peel, and lemongrass to a tea ball, then place it in room-temperature water. Allow the tea to brew for 10 minutes, moving the tea ball from time to time. Once brewed, remove the tea ball from the water.
2. In a shaker, add 3 ½ oz of the tea base with the agave, pineapple juice, and vodka. Shake until the agave dissolves fully.
3. Add the ice to a glass, pour the tea mixture over the ice, and stir gently to chill the mixture.
4. Garnish with the pineapple wedge and serve chilled.

Marry Me

Servings: 1

Prep Time: 15 minutes

Ingredients:

Tea Base

- 6 oz water, room temperature
- ¼ tsp dried basil
- ¾ tsp rooibos tea leaves

Cocktail

- 1 tbsp agave
- 1 ½ oz tequila
- 4 ½ oz tea base
- ice
- 1 fresh basil leaf

Directions:

1. To make the tea base, add the dried basil and rooibos tea leaves to a tea ball, then place it in room-temperature water. Allow the tea to brew for 10 minutes, moving the tea ball from time to time. Once brewed, remove the tea ball from the water.
2. In a shaker, add 4 ½ oz of the tea base, the agave, and the tequila. Shake until the agave is fully dissolved.
3. Add the ice to the shaker and swirl gently to chill the mixture.
4. Strain the mixture into a glass with the ice.
5. Garnish with the fresh basil and serve chilled.

Ginger Peach

Servings: 1

Prep Time: 15 minutes

Ingredients:

Tea Base

- 6 oz water, room temperature
- ½ tsp ground ginger
- ¾ tsp dried peach
- ¾ tsp green tea leaves

Cocktail

- 1 tbsp agave
- 1 ½ oz mescal
- 4 ½ oz tea base
- ice
- candied ginger

Directions:

1. To make the tea base, add the ground ginger, dried peach, and green tea leaves to a tea ball, then place it in room-temperature water. Allow

the tea to brew for 10 minutes, moving the tea ball from time to time. Once brewed, remove the tea ball from the water.

2. In a shaker, combine 4 ½ oz of the tea base with the agave and mescal. Shake until the agave has dissolved completely.
3. Add the ice to a glass, pour the cocktail over the ice, and stir gently to chill the mixture.
4. Garnish with the candied ginger and serve chilled.

Bloody Tea

Servings: 4

Prep Time: 20 minutes

Ingredients:

Tea Base

- 6 oz water, room temperature
- 2 tsp Assam tea leaves

Cocktail

- 4 oz red wine
- 4 oz tequila

- 4 oz tea base
- 16 oz sweetened tomato juice
- 4 dashes hot sauce
- 5 dashes Worcestershire sauce
- 2 pinches black pepper
- 2 pinches celery salt
- 2 pinches salt
- ice
- olives
- lime wedges

Directions:

1. To make the tea base, add the Assam tea leaves to a tea ball, then place it in room-temperature water. Allow the tea to brew for 10 minutes, moving the tea ball from time to time. Once brewed, remove the tea ball from the water.
2. In a large jug, mix together the red wine, tequila, tomato juice, hot sauce, Worcestershire sauce, black pepper, celery salt, and salt.
3. Add 4 oz of the tea base and stir gently.
4. Add the ice to the glasses, then pour the mixture over the ice.
5. Garnish each glass with the olives and lime wedges and serve chilled.

White Sangria

Servings: 4

Prep Time: 20 minutes

Ingredients:

Tea Base

- 13 oz water, room temperature
- ¼ tsp dried lemon peel
- ¾ tsp dried peach
- ½ tsp lemongrass, chopped
- ½ tsp white tea leaves

Cocktail

- ¼ cup agave
- 12 oz white wine
- 12 oz tea base
- ice
- fresh peach slices

Directions:

1. To make the tea base, add the lemongrass, dried peach, dried lemon peel, and white tea leaves to

two tea balls. Make sure that there are equal amounts of the ingredients in each tea ball.

2. Place the tea balls in room-temperature water and allow the tea to brew for 10 minutes, moving the tea balls from time to time. Once brewed, remove the tea balls from the water.
3. In a large jug, add the agave, white wine, and 12 oz of the tea base. Stir well until the agave is fully dissolved.
4. Add the peach slices to the jug and place the mixture in the fridge to chill for at least an hour.
5. Serve over ice.

Dirty Chai

Servings: 1

Prep Time: 15 minutes

Ingredients:

Tea Base

- 6 oz water, room temperature
- a pinch of dried jasmine flowers
- 2 tsp masala chai

Cocktail

- ½ tbsp agave
- ½ oz elderflower liqueur (you can use rose water if you prefer)
- 1 oz sloe gin
- 2 oz white wine
- 3 ½ oz tea base
- 2 oz soda water
- ice

Directions:

1. To make the tea base, add the dried jasmine flowers and the masala chai to a tea ball, then place it in room-temperature water. Allow the tea to brew for 10 minutes, moving the tea ball from time to time. Once brewed, remove the tea ball from the water.
2. In a shaker, combine 3 ½ oz of the tea base with the agave, elderflower liqueur, sloe gin, and white wine. Shake until the agave is dissolved.
3. Add the ice to a glass, then pour the mixture over the ice.
4. Add the soda water to the iced mixture and swirl gently to chill before enjoying.

Green Fun

Servings: 1

Prep Time: 15 minutes

Ingredients:

Tea Base

- 6 oz water, room temperature
- ½ tsp dried peach
- ½ tsp ground ginger
- ½ tsp yerba maté
- ½ tsp green tea leaves

Cocktail

- 1 tbsp agave
- 1 ½ oz tequila
- 4 ½ oz tea base
- ice
- 1 ginger slice

Directions:

1. To make the tea base, add the dried peach, ginger, yerba maté, and green tea leaves to a tea

ball then place it in room-temperature water. Allow the tea to brew for 10 minutes, moving the tea ball from time to time. Once brewed, remove the tea ball from the water.

2. In a shaker, add the agave, tequila, and 3 ½ oz of the tea base. Shake until the agave dissolves fully.
3. Add the ice to the shaker and stir gently to chill the mixture.
4. Strain the cocktail into a glass and garnish with the ginger slice before serving.

Chocolate Valentine

Servings: 1

Prep Time: 15 minutes

Ingredients:

Tea Base

- 6 oz water, room temperature
- 2 tsp green tea leaves
- 2 tsp unsweetened coconut, shredded
- 2 tsp vanilla beans
- 2 tsp chai spice
- 2 tsp dried fig, chopped

Cocktail

- 1 oz Kahlúa
- 1 tbsp agave
- 3 oz brewed tea base
- 3 oz champagne
- ice

Directions:

1. To make the tea base, add the green tea leaves, coconut, vanilla, chai spice, and dried fig to a bowl. Mix well to combine. You will have more than you need, so you can store the extra in an airtight container for later.
2. Add 2 tsp of the tea mixture to a tea ball, then place it in the water. Allow this to brew for 10 minutes, moving the tea ball from time to time. Once brewed, remove the tea ball from the water.
3. To a shaker, add the Kahlúa, agave, and 3 oz of the tea base. Shake well until the agave is dissolved.
4. Add the ice to the shaker and gently mix to chill. Pour the champagne over the ice and swirl again.
5. Pour into a glass and serve chilled.

Strawberry Sparkle

Servings: 1

Prep Time: 15 minutes

Ingredients:

Tea Base

- 6 oz water, room temperature
- 1 tsp rose petals, dried
- 1 tsp strawberries, dried

Cocktail

- 1 oz elderflower liqueur
- 3 oz tea base
- 3 oz champagne
- ice

Directions:

1. To make the tea base, add the rose petals and strawberries to a tea ball, then place it in room-temperature water. Allow the tea to brew for 10 minutes, moving the tea ball from time to time. Once brewed, remove the tea ball from the water.

2. In a shaker, add the elderflower liqueur and 3 oz of the tea base. Shake to combine.
3. Add the ice to the shaker and stir gently to chill the mixture.
4. Strain the cocktail into a glass, then top it with the champagne before serving.

CONCLUSION

When you hold that warm cup of tea in your hand and take those first deep inhales, you are transported to a whole new place. You can feel your body relaxing and your senses becoming less overwhelmed. You soften and unwind. It is as if that cup of tea triggers your body to calm down and shed its burdens, even for a few minutes. It is one of my favorite moments in my day. My tea ritual has become part of my daily life, and I'm better for it. We each drink tea for a different reason, and we each have a story that connects us to our tea ritual, but I truly believe we all experience that moment of sheer pleasure when we take that first sip.

Tea has a long history. It has the power to heal and incite wars, but it remains one of the world's most produced and traded goods. Almost every culture in the world has a ritual around tea, probably because they recognize that the simple act of making tea has physical, emotional, and mental benefits.

The world of tea is varied and exciting. Each variety of tea brings different flavor profiles and scents and can elicit varying sensations or even emotions. Each cup of tea is singular in its taste because it reflects you as the tea maker. You define how your tea should be. I've just provided the basic guidelines to help you get started in the vast world of tea. I'm still experimenting and experiencing. I may have begun with herbal teas, but my eyes and taste buds have opened to so much more since I started. I can only wish the same for you.

YOUR ADVENTURE AWAITS

I hope the recipes and stories shared in this book have been as exciting for you to read as they were for me to write. If you've made it this far, I know that you're ready to jump right in if you haven't already. Tea is versatile. It can bring joy or comfort. You can reach for a cup of tea in celebration and despair. Tea is personal, and there is no right or wrong way to make your tea.

The recipes in this book are just a place for you to start, find what works best for you, experiment, and have fun. Tea is never boring. There are always new flavors, aromas, and textures to be experienced. You can create your own blends based on your mood or your body's needs or as a gift for a friend. The possibilities are truly endless.

My sincerest hope is that you are inspired to find your own tea adventure, delve deeper into creating your own tea rituals and stories, and share your passion with others. So where will your adventure take you?

REFERENCES

A Thirst for Tea, Inc (n.d.). *Nantou Dong Ding oolong preparation.* https://www.athirstfortea.com/pages/dong-ding-preparation

Adamant, A. (2018, August 31). *How to make the perfect cup of echinacea tea.* Practical Self Reliance. https://practicalselfreliance.com/echinacea-tea/

Ali. (2018, April 6). *5-minute iced rooibos latte.* Gimme Some Oven. https://www.gimmesomeoven.com/5-minute-iced-rooibos-latte/#tasty-recipes-60557

Art of Tea. (n.d.-a). *Self-care guide: The healing powers of tea.* https://www.artoftea.com/blogs/health-lifestyle/self-care-guide-the-healing-powers-of-tea

Art of Tea. (n.d.-b). *What is black tea?* https://www.artoftea.com/blogs/tea-101/what-is-black-tea

Art of Tea. (n.d.-c). *What is Pu-erh tea?* https://www.artoftea.com/blogs/tea-101/what-is-pu-erh-tea#:~:text=Pu%2Derh%20tea%20can%20be

Bauer, E. (2022, November 25). *Agua de Jamaica (hibiscus iced tea).* Simply Recipes. https://www.simplyrecipes.com/recipes/agua_de_jamaica_hibiscus_tea/

Begum, R. (2017, May 24). *Rose, citrus, berry and apple homemade tea.* The Delicious Crescent. https://www.thedeliciouscrescent.com/rose-dried-fruit-homemade-tea/

Born Tea. (n.d.). *Complete guide to white tea.* https://www.borntea.com/blogs/tea/complete-guide-to-white-tea

Brown, M. J. (2018, November 13). *5 health benefits of rooibos tea (plus side effects).* Healthline. https://www.healthline.com/nutrition/rooibos-tea-benefits

Choe, J. (2020a, April 26). *How to make Assam tea properly (hot & iced).* Oh, How Civilized. https://www.ohhowcivilized.com/assam-tea/

Choe, J. (2020b, May 1). *Cold brew tea: What it is & how to make it prop-*

erly. Oh, How Civilized. https://www.ohhowcivilized.com/make-best-iced-tea-cold-brew/

Choe, J. (2020c, May 29). *How to make Ceylon tea properly (hot & iced).* Oh, How Civilized. https://www.ohhowcivilized.com/ceylon-tea/

Choe, J. (2020d, August 9). *How to make Lapsang souchong properly (hot & iced).* Oh, How Civilized. https://www.ohhowcivilized.com/lasang-souchong-tea/

Chung, L. (2021, January 23). *Chinese famous green tea: Biluochun, step to step brew guide.* Leo Tea World. https://leoteaworld.com/2021/01/23/chinese-famous-green-tea-biluochun-step-to-step-brew-guide/

Denby, L. (2022, September 2). *All the tools you need to brew perfect tea, according to the pros.* Forbes. https://www.forbes.com/sites/forbes-personal-shopper/2022/09/22/tea-tools-essentials-teapot-kettle/?sh=75018ca16720

Diana's Desserts. (2003, March 28). *Keemun tea.* Diana's Desserts. http://www.dianasdesserts.com/index.cfm/fuseaction/recipes.recipeListing/filter/dianas/recipeID/1426/Recipe.cfm

Donofrio, J. (2020, April 17). *Matcha 101: What it is and how to use it.* Love and Lemons. https://www.loveandlemons.com/matcha-green-tea/

Edward, M. (2019, November 15). *What does peppermint tea taste like?* Tea in Abstraction. https://teainabstraction.com/what-does-pepper mint-tea-taste-like/

Elliott, B. (2017, August 18). *5 ways chamomile tea benefits your health.* Healthline. https://www.healthline.com/nutrition/5-benefits-of-chamomile-tea

Falkowitz, M. (2022, July 21). *A beginner's guide to drinking better oolong tea.* Serious Eats. https://www.seriouseats.com/what-is-oolong-tea-where-to-buy

Farr, S. (2016). *Healing herbal teas: Learn to blend 101 specially formulated teas for stress management, common ailments, seasonal health, and immune support.* Storey Publishing.

Farrer's. (2020, September 10). *Top 10 tea producing countries in the world 2021.* John Farrer & Co (Kendal) Ltd. https://farrerscoffee.co.uk/blogs/blog/top-10-tea-producing-countries-in-the-world-2021

Fountaine, S. (2019, January 2). *Delicious authentic masala chai with whole spices.* Feasting at Home. https://www.feastingathome.com/authentic-masala-chai-recipe/#tasty-recipes-26588-jump-target

Frey, M. (2021, October 12). *The health benefits of echinacea.* Verywell Fit. https://www.verywellfit.com/echinacea-tea-benefits-and-side-effects-4163612

Friends. (2014, December 28). *New year tea blend recipe with white peony and cedar berries.* Mountain Rose Herbs. https://blog.mountainroseherbs.com/sunday-steep-40

Gaumont, S. (n.d.). *Irish breakfast tea: Tasting and brewing guide.* Tea Backyard. https://teabackyard.com/irish-breakfast-tea/

Goodwin, L. (2022a, June 24). *The history of masala chai.* The Spruce Eats. https://www.thespruceeats.com/the-history-of-masala-chai-tea-765836

Goodwin, L. (2022b, July 14). *Make refreshing mint tea with this easy recipe.* The Spruce Eats. https://www.thespruceeats.com/easy-fresh-mint-tea-recipe-766391

Goodwin, L. (2022c, September 8). *What is sencha green tea? Benefits, uses, & recipes.* The Spruce Eats. https://www.thespruceeats.com/sencha-765146

Goodwin, L. (2022d, September 20). *Pu-erh: Why you need to try this rare tea.* The Spruce Eats. https://www.thespruceeats.com/what-is-pu-erh-tea-766434

Hackett, J. (2022, June 30). *Soothe yourself with delicious homemade ginger tea.* The Spruce Eats. https://www.thespruceeats.com/homemade-ginger-tea-3377239

Hannah. (2018, January 3). *DIY rooibos tea blends.* Mountain Rose Herbs. https://blog.mountainroseherbs.com/rooibos-tea-blends

Harvard Health Publishing. (2021, October 21). *The health benefits of 3 herbal teas.* https://www.health.harvard.edu/nutrition/the-health-benefits-of-3-herbal-teas

Joi Tea. (n.d.). *The art of brewing tea.* https://joitea.co.nz/blogs/articles/the-art-of-brewing-tea

Joshua. (2022, November 19). *Boba Buddha's Assam milk tea recipe.* Bobabuddha. https://bobabuddha.com/assam-milk-tea-recipe/

JUSTEA. (n.d.). *Everything you didn't know about tea in Kenya.* https://justea.com/blogs/tea-101/everything-you-didn-t-know-about-tea-in-kenya

Karma Tea Co. (2022, July 27). *Assam iced tea.* https://www.karmateaco.com/blogs/news/assam-iced-tea

Lang, A. (2022, February 22). *Ginger tea benefits: Nausea, pain relief, and blood sugar.* Healthline. https://www.healthline.com/nutrition/benefits-ginger-tea#potential-downsides

Lapcevic, K. (2019, October 25). *Ginger lemon balm green tea blend.* Homespun Seasonal Living. https://homespunseasonalliving.com/ginger-lemon-balm-green-tea-blend/#mv-creation-168-jtr

Levinson, J. (2022, July 27). *Health benefits of hibiscus tea, according to a dietitian.* EatingWell. https://www.eatingwell.com/article/7989695/health-benefits-of-hibiscus-tea-according-to-a-dietitian/

Link, R. (2022, November 21). *8 benefits of hibiscus tea.* Healthline. https://www.healthline.com/nutrition/hibiscus-tea-benefits

Lotusier. (n.d.). *Journey of tea.* https://lotusier.com/journey-of-tea

Marie. (2018, January 10). *Honey ginger cinnamon latte.* Yay! For Food. https://www.yayforfood.com/recipes/honey-ginger-cinnamon-latte/#mv-creation-116-jtr

Meghan. (2021, December 13). *Why grandpa style tea brewing is the best way to enjoy tea.* Afternoon Tea Reads. https://afternoonteareads.com/why-grandpa-style-is-the-best-way-to-enjoy-tea/

Mei Leaf. (2022, December 21). *Laoshan green.* https://meileaf.com/tea/laoshan-green/

Mistry, M. (2021, December 15). *How the ancient art of making tea became modern self-care.* Town & Country. https://www.townandcountrymag.com/leisure/a38279498/tea-ceremony-social-history/

Miyuki. (2022, January 12). *Easy DIY vanilla rooibos tea blend.* Dreamy Cup. https://www.dreamycup.com/easy-diy-vanilla-rooibos-tea-blend/#recipe

My Japanese Green Tea. (n.d.). *Gyokuro.* https://www.myjapanesegreentea.com/gyokuro

Nio Teas. (2022, July 26). *Everything you need to know about sencha.* https://nioteas.com/blogs/sencha/sencha-complete-guide

Overhiser, S. (2021, August 7). *How to make matcha (Japanese green tea).* A Couple Cooks. https://www.acouplecooks.com/how-to-make-matcha/

Path of Cha. (n.d.-a). *Basic guidelines for brewing a good cup of tea (7 easy steps).* https://pathofcha.com/pages/basic-principles-for-brewing-a-good-cup-of-tea

Path of Cha. (n.d.-b). *How to brew tea: The 5 methods.* https://pathofcha.com/blogs/all-about-tea/how-to-brew-tea-the-5-methods

Prakash, S. (2020, January 29). *Recipe: Honey chamomile tea latte.* Kitchn. https://www.thekitchn.com/honey-chamomile-tea-latte-264565

Raman, R. (2018, October 25). *Echinacea: Benefits, uses, side effects and dosage.* Healthline. https://www.healthline.com/nutrition/echinacea

Randolph, L. (2019). *Your guide to white tea: Caffeine levels, taste and more.* The Spruce Eats. https://www.thespruceeats.com/what-is-white-tea-766437

Rardon, C. R. (2020). *Stuff every tea lover should know.* Quirk Books.

Revolution Tea. (n.d.-a). *The beginners' guide to Lapsang souchong – Everything you should know.* https://www.revolutiontea.com/blogs/news/the-beginners-guide-to-lapsang-souchong

Revolution Tea. (n.d.-b). *The history of green tea.* https://www.revolutiontea.com/blogs/news/the-history-of-green-tea

Richa. (2021, June 24). *How to make hibiscus tea + its benefits.* My Food Story. https://myfoodstory.com/hibiscus-tea-recipe/#recipe

Ripps, J., & Littlefield, M. (2015). *Wise cocktails.* Rodale Books.

Rosie Loves Tea. (2020, June 19). *Iced Darjeeling tea with fresh oranges.* https://www.rosielovestea.com/recipes/2020/6/18/iced-darjeeling-with-fresh-oranges

Samira. (2022, April 12). *How to make chamomile tea.* Alphafoodie. https://www.alphafoodie.com/how-to-make-chamomile-tea/#recipe-tips-and-notes

Sandoval, M. (2019, June 10). *Cinnamon orange black tea recipe.* Tasty. https://tasty.co/recipe/cinnamon-orange-black-tea

Senbird Tea. (n.d.). *Genmaicha.* https://senbirdtea.com/teatype/genmaicha-brown-rice-green-tea/

Sencha Tea Bar. (n.d.-a). *Dragon's well tea: The ultimate guide to Longjing tea.* https://senchateabar.com/blogs/blog/dragons-well-tea

Sencha Tea Bar. (n.d.-b). *The history of tea: Steeped in legend, admired in politics, and consumed in abundance.* https://senchateabar.com/blogs/blog/history-of-tea

Sencha Tea Bar. (n.d.-c). *The ultimate guide to Da Hong Pao tea.* https://senchateabar.com/blogs/blog/da-hong-pao

Simple Loose Leaf. (2020a, April 1). *What is Keemun tea? Top black teas to try, brewing tips.* https://simplelooseleaf.com/blog/black-tea/keemun-tea/

Simple Loose Leaf. (2020b, July 12). *What is Tieguanyin tea? Complete guide to health benefits, effects, brewing.* https://simplelooseleaf.com/blog/oolong-tea/tieguanyin-tea/

Simple Loose Leaf. (2021a, April 7). *English breakfast tea recipes: New, delicious twists on a classic tea base.* https://simplelooseleaf.com/blog/black-tea/english-breakfast-tea-recipe/

Simple Loose Leaf. (2021b, April 20). *Pouchong tea guide: Health benefits, caffeine, best taste.* https://simplelooseleaf.com/blog/oolong-tea/pouchong-tea-guide/

Sivasubramaniam, S. (2019). *Tea.* Encyclopædia Britannica. https://www.britannica.com/topic/tea-beverage

Sonia. (2018, May 7). *Pu-erh tea blends: 8 ways to spice up pu-erh.* Hello Tea Cup. https://helloteacup.com/2018/05/07/pu-erh-tea-blends/

Steven Smith Teamaker. (n.d.). *How to brew pu-erh teas.* https://www.smithtea.com/pages/how-to-brew-pu-erh-tea

Szaro, M. (2022, May 27). *How to make your own tea blends and a soothing sleep tea recipe.* Herbal Academy. https://theherbalacademy.com/tea-blends/

Tara. (2017, May 30). *Chai ya tangawizi (Kenyan ginger tea).* Tara's Multicultural Table. https://tarasmulticulturaltable.com/chai-ya-tangawizi-kenyan-ginger-tea/

Tea Adventures. (2021, October 30). *How to brew tea: Western style.* https://tea-adventures.net/tea-education/western-style/

Tea Association of the USA Inc. (2022). *Tea fact sheet 2022.* https://www.teausa.com/teausa/images/Tea_Fact_2021.pdf

Tea Cachai. (2021a, October 1). *Caffeine in white tea: Myth-busting and facts.* https://www.teacachai.com/caffeine-in-white-tea/

Tea Cachai. (2021b, October 1). *Top 7 tea tools and accessories.* https://www.teacachai.com/top-7-tea-tools-and-accessories/

Tea Coffee Basket. (2022, April 8). *Sunburst Darjeeling tea.* https://www.teacoffeebasket.com/sunburst-darjeeling-tea/

Tea Forte. (2021, August 26). *5 secrets to the perfect cup of Earl Grey tea.* https://teaforte.com/blogs/tea-notes/5-secrets-to-the-perfect-cup-of-earl-grey-tea

Tea Sprig. (n.d.). *The principles of tea brewing.* https://teasprig.com/the-principles-of-tea-brewing/

Teasenz. (2016, April 4). *White tea legend: The lazy Xiao brother's Shou Mei/Gong Mei discovery.* https://www.teasenz.com/chinese-tea/white-tea-legend-shou-mei.html

Teasenz. (2019a, August 4). *The origin of oolong tea (or "wulong tea").* https://www.teasenz.com/chinese-tea/the-origin-of-oolong-tea.html

Teasenz. (2019b, September 30). *Dan Cong oolong tea: Legend, history & origin.* https://www.teasenz.com/chinese-tea/dan-cong-oolong-tea-legend-history-origin.html

Teasenz. (2022, May 11). *Legend of Da Hong Pao tea: Tales & mother trees.* https://www.teasenz.com/chinese-tea/legend-da-hong-pao-tea.html

TeaTime. (2015, June 9). *Iced Irish tea.* https://www.teatimemagazine.com/iced-irish-tea-recipe/

Teavivre. (n.d.-a). *Guide to brew Silver Needle white tea properly.* https://www.teavivre.com/info/brewing-silver-needle-tea.html

Teavivre. (n.d.-b). *The guide to making white tea: How to brew White Peony Bai Mu Dan tea.* https://www.teavivre.com/info/guide-to-making-white-peony-tea.html

The Fragrant Leaf. (n.d.). *Bai Hao Oolong tea: Taiwan's beauty.* https://thefragrantleaf.com/pages/bai-hao-oolong-taiwans-beauty

The Tao of Tea. (n.d.-a). *Baihao Oolong.* https://taooftea.com/product/baihao-oolong/

The Tao of Tea. (n.d.-b). *White Darjeeling.* https://taooftea.com/prod

uct/white-darjeeling/

Tiwari, A. (2020, April 27). *Assam milk tea recipe: Know all about how to make Assam milk tea.* Teafloor Blog. https://teafloor.com/blog/how-to-make-assam-milk-tea/

Tiwari, A. (2021, April 18). *Darjeeling tea recipe | 5 amazing recipes you must know.* Teafloor. https://teafloor.com/blog/darjeeling-tea-5-amazing-recipes-you-must-know/

Tranquil Tuesdays. (n.d.). *Five simple principles for making the perfect cup of tea.* https://www.tranquiltuesdays.com/resource-library/five-simple-principles-for-making-the-perfect-cup-of-tea

Trident. (n.d.). *Laoshan Chinese green tea.* https://www.tridentcafe.com/green/laoshan-green

Tulali, R. (2022, February 17). *The in-depth guide to Silver Needle white tea.* Tea Curious. https://www.teacurious.com/guide-silver-needle

27teas. (2019, September 20). *Gong Fu vs. Western style brewing.* https://27teas.com/2019/09/20/gong-fu-vs-western-style/

Uhl, J. (2015). *The art and craft of tea: An enthusiast's guide to selecting, brewing, and serving exquisite tea.* Quarry Books.

Venison for Dinner. (2020, December 30). *DIY loose leaf raspberry hibiscus green tea blend.* https://venisonfordinner.com/2020/12/30/diy-loose-leaf-raspberry-hibiscus-green-tea-blend/#recipe

Vicony Teas. (n.d.). *How to brew Longjing tea (dragon well).* https://www.viconyteas.com/directory/tea-encyclopedia/brew-longjing.html

WAWAZA. (n.d.). *How to brew a perfect cup of sencha tea in 4 easy steps.* https://wawaza.com/pages/how-to-brew-a-perfect-cup-of-japanese-sencha-green-tea/

WebMD Editorial Contributors. (2022, November 22). *Mint tea: Health benefits, nutrition facts, and how to prepare it.* WebMD. https://www.webmd.com/diet/mint-tea-health-benefits

Wilkinson, I. (2018, November 12). *What is Yunnan black tea?* Good & Proper Tea. https://www.goodandpropertea.com/blogs/all/what-is-yunnan-black-tea

Wilson, S. (2020, September 28). *How to brew Earl Grey tea.* 31 Daily. https://www.31daily.com/how-to-brew-earl-grey-tea/

Wilson, S. (2021, March 17). *How to brew Irish Breakfast tea.* 31 Daily. https://www.31daily.com/how-to-brew-irish-breakfast-tea/

Yellow Mountain Tea House. (n.d.). *Feng Huang Dan Cong oolong tea.* https://www.yellow-mountain-organic-tea.com/products/copy-of-copy-of-osmanthus-oolong-tea

Yuki. (2021a, November 18). *How to brew the perfect cup of Genmaicha.* TeaLife. https://japanesetea.sg/japanese-tea-pedia/how-to-brew-delicious-genmaicha/

Yuki. (2021b, November 22). *7 steps to making the perfect cup of Gyokuro tea.* TeaLife. https://japanesetea.sg/japanese-tea-pedia/how-to-brew-delicious-gyokuro/

Zlobinski, S. (2020, October 28). *How to brew pu-erh tea.* Just Puerh. https://www.justpuerh.ca/blogs/blog/how-to-brew-pu-erh-tea

Made in the USA
Columbia, SC
24 September 2024

2fcb6f61-fe1e-4ea2-a9d2-536f46486d6eR01